The Hike Life
50 MORE TO EXPLORE

Black&White

First published in the UK in 2024 by
Black & White Publishing Ltd
Nautical House, 104 Commercial Street, Edinburgh, EH6 6NF

A division of Bonnier Books UK
4th Floor, Victoria House, Bloomsbury Square, London, WC1B 4DA
Owned by Bonnier Books, Sveavägen 56, Stockholm, Sweden

Copyright © Rozanna Purcell 2024
Illustrated icons used under license by stock.adobe.com
All image credits listed on page 278

All rights reserved. No part of this publication may be reproduced, stored or transmitted in any form by any means, electronic, mechanical, photocopying or otherwise, without the prior written permission of the publisher.

The right of Rozanna Purcell to be identified as Author of this work has been asserted by her in accordance with the Copyright, Designs and Patents Act, 1988.

The Hike Life isn't a guide to hiking safety and therefore neither the author nor the publisher can accept any responsibility for damage of any kind, to property or persons, that occurs either directly or indirectly from the use of this book or from any hiking or water-based activity.

A CIP catalogue record for this book is available from the British Library.

ISBN: 978 1 78530 699 0

1 3 5 7 9 10 8 6 4 2

Layout by Black & White
Printed and bound in Latvia

www.blackandwhitepublishing.com

The Hike Life
50 MORE TO EXPLORE
MY FAVOURITE HIKES IN IRELAND

ROZANNA PURCELL

Black&White

This book is dedicated to my Aunt Mary, who passed away recently. My first ever hike was with Mary. I was too young to remember, but I have the photos to prove it. All through my childhood she marched me and my sisters up Sliabh na mBan, despite our moaning and complaining! As well as my love for the mountains, she gave me my love of baking and supporting Tipperary GAA. So here's to Mary, and all of the other aunts, sisters and mothers who encourage a love of the outdoors and pass on their passions whatever they may be.

ADVICE TO READERS

Please note that the trail described in each hike is not for navigational purposes but merely to give an overall idea of the route, terrain and points of interest along the way. Always use appropriate navigational tools when hiking. Every effort has been made by the author to ensure that the content of this book is as accurate and up-to-date as possible at the time of going to press. However, it is important to note that changes can occur over time to transport routes, rights of way, access, and in other ways. It therefore remains the reader's sole responsibility to check and verify all information independently before setting out. If you do find there have been any changes to a route mentioned in this book, e.g. a route is closed or a route is no longer dog friendly, please email the details to mail@blackandwhitepublishing.com.

WARNING

Both hiking and wild swimming can be hazardous activities which can carry the risk of personal injury or death. These activities require planning, knowledge and experience, and should only be undertaken by those with suitable training and understanding of the risks involved. This book is intended as a guide only, and it remains the responsibility of all users to make themselves aware of the risks involved. In particular, weather conditions on the hills and mountains of Ireland can change very quickly at any time of year, and this can have a material effect on any hill or mountain walk. Before wild swimming, be aware of your surroundings, water temperature and conditions, including any tides or currents, and make sure it is safe to continue. Check the water quality status of the area, and familiarise yourself with swimming safety, including what to do when things go wrong.

Neither the publisher nor the author can accept any liability whatsoever for any damage of any kind, including damage to property, or personal injury or death, arising either directly or indirectly from the information in this book.

Anyone undertaking a hill or mountain walk, or any form of climbing excursion, should familiarise themselves with the number for Mountain Rescue. Additionally, anyone undertaking any form of wild swimming should familiarise themselves with safe swimming guidelines and the RNLI's Float to Live guide. If you find yourself or someone else in difficulty, dial 112 (Ireland) or 999 (NI) and ask for the relevant authority. The emergency operator can then direct your call.

The Hike Life
50 MORE TO EXPLORE

Introduction 1
Preparing for your hike 5
Wildlife 14
Apps and websites 16
Leave no trace 18
Ticks 20
Terminology 22
Difficulty levels 25
Hiking list 28

CONNACHT
Tully Mountain 33
Benlettery 37
Benbaun 43
Mount Gable 47
Slievemore 51
Wild Nephin National Park 55
Erris Head Loop 59
Union Rock 63
Devil's Chimney Waterfall 67
Benbulbin 71
Mullaghgarve Mass Rock 77

LEINSTER
Bray Head and Hill 83
Cruagh Wood 89
Scarr Mountain 93
Devil's Glen 97
Luggala Mountain 101
Derrybawn Mountain 105
Turlough Hill, Camaderry and
  St Kevins Way Loop 111
Sorrel Hill 115
Glen Beach Cliff Walk 121
Mount Leinster and Slieve Bawn 125
Raven Wood Nature Reserve 131
Portrane to Donabate Coastal Walk 135
Mullaghmeen 139

MUNSTER
Cruach Mhárthain 145
Sauce Creek 149
Strickeen Mountain from Gap of Dunloe 155
Derrycunnihy Church to Lord Brandon's
  Cottage Mass Path 161
Bray Head, Valentia 165
Knocknadobar 169
Gleninchaquin Park 173
Hungry Hill 177
Three Castle Head 183
Knockomagh 187
Ardmore Cliff Walk 193
Nire Valley Trails 197
The Devil's Bit 201
Moylussa 205
Kilkee Cliff Walk and Loop Head 209
Abbey Hill 215

ULSTER
Urris Lakes Loop 221
Knockalla Ridge 227
Horn Head 233
An Port to Glenlough Bay 237
Fair Head 243
Ben Crom 249
Tollymore Forest 253
Hen Mountain 259
Slieve Martin and Kodak Corner 265
Slieve Gullion 271

Acknowledgements 275
About the author 277
Image credits 278

INTRODUCTION

I have always loved the outdoors, inspired by growing up in the shadows of Sliabh na mBan, County Tipperary. No matter where I have lived in my life since then, I have always been drawn to mountains for adventure, escape, fitness and to explore my love of photography. Sharing this through social and traditional media led to the creation of The Hike Life community in 2018. My mission with The Hike Life is to get more people exploring, appreciating and respecting our outdoor spaces. The Hike Life community has become a space where people can join events, find hiking inspiration for Ireland and abroad, and meet other like-minded people. One of my greatest pleasures in creating The Hike Life community is seeing more women taking to the trails. This led me to establish the Women in the Great Outdoors Initiative, offering free upskilling courses to female hikers, and supporting some to become mountain leaders. This wonderful journey led me to create *The Hike Life* books.

HIKING IN IRELAND

Ireland is a treasure trove for hikers: for a small country we have so many amazing outdoor spaces. The Irish landscape is also relatively untouched, allowing you to really appreciate the geography and geology of each area.

But I always say, the best thing about hiking in Ireland is the people you meet. Whether it's a simple hello, or encouragement to push on to the summit, the hikers in Ireland are the friendliest of anywhere I have been. Hiking is an incredibly popular activity in Ireland, and you will meet people of all ages on the trails. Ireland also has a good network of qualified mountain leaders, who will not only guide you on the trail, but will regale you with stories on the way. There are lots of mountaineering and hiking clubs in Ireland, which can be a great way to meet like-minded people in your own area. Improvements to the trails are being made all the time, and the number of marked trails is increasing every year, as are the facilities at popular hiking destinations, such as parking and toilets.

ABOUT THIS BOOK

The first *Hike Life* book showcased some of the best hikes on the island of Ireland, including Ireland's highest peak, our most well-known mountains and some of our most popular trails. Most importantly, it encouraged lots of people to get outside and explore what Ireland has to offer. This book is a continuation of my favourite hikes in Ireland, including some more well-known mountains and trails, but also hidden gems that I am excited to introduce to you.

This book covers the four provinces of Ireland and offers a variety of trails, including mountain and forest trails, and coastal hikes. Each hike includes information on local points of interest, recommendations for other activities to do, places to eat and swim spots, all in the vicinity of the trail. The general statistics for each hike are presented, as is a general overview of the route. I also identify the hikes that are dog friendly, as well as practical information about parking.

This book has everything you loved about *The Hike Life* (book 1), with some additions.

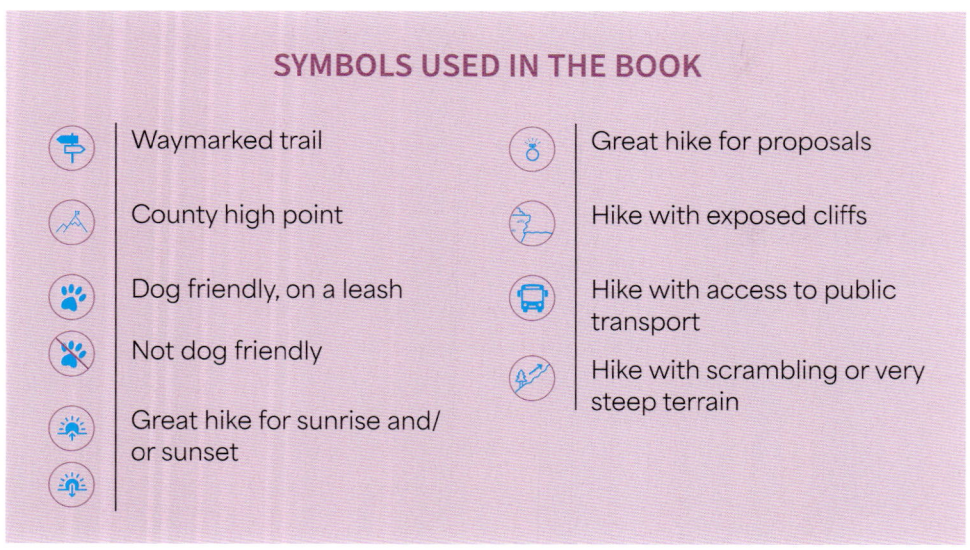

SYMBOLS USED IN THE BOOK

- Waymarked trail
- County high point
- Dog friendly, on a leash
- Not dog friendly
- Great hike for sunrise and/or sunset
- Great hike for proposals
- Hike with exposed cliffs
- Hike with access to public transport
- Hike with scrambling or very steep terrain

PREPARING FOR YOUR HIKE

Hiking brings you to amazing places, but these same places are vast, remote and difficult to access if something goes wrong. So, it is important to hike smart and consider your safety and those who may need to come to your rescue should something go wrong.

Check the difficulty rating, elevation, distance and terrain of your planned route, check the weather forecast and use all this information to assess the level of skill and equipment required, and whether it is appropriate for you.

The best way to ensure your safety and enjoyment on a hike, especially difficult hikes, is to book an experienced mountain leader to guide you, and I have listed some of my recommendations for each hike marked hard or above. I also highly recommend taking a mountain skills course to better your knowledge and skills for hillwalking. You can find a list of course providers in your area at mountaineering.ie.

Here are some other tips to help you hike smart.

HYDRATION AND NUTRITION

Ensuring you have adequate hydration and nutrition for the hike is essential. A general rule of thumb for hydration is 250ml for every 30 minutes of hiking, but this will change depending on weather conditions and hike intensity. For easy and moderate hikes, nutrition is a point of personal preference and influenced by the time of day, and your consumption before setting off. Personally, I think it's always a good idea to have some emergency food in your hiking bag – for example, an energy ball, a protein bar, or some jellies for a quick burst of energy. For more difficult hikes, bringing nutrition is essential. Anything that you enjoy and travels well in a hiking bag will work – always ensure any rubbish comes back with you.

LAYERING

Layering your hiking clothing is the key to controlling your temperature, whether that's keeping warm or cooling off. Layering offers hikers an easy way to be prepared for and adjust to the conditions as they change. Ideally, each layer should be fitted to trap warm air. The number of layers will obviously be determined by the conditions you are facing on a particular day, and you may opt to carry some lightweight layers in your rucksack until needed. From the inside out, the three basic hiking clothing layers are:

BASE LAYER	Tank top, T-shirt, or long-sleeve top and bottoms. Preferably made from a synthetic moisture-wicking material or wool.
INSULATING LAYER	This could be a fleece, insulated jacket, or both.
WEATHERPROOF LAYER	Waterproof and windproof jacket/bottoms.

Before your hike

- Make sure any online maps are downloaded while you have phone reception.
- Save local mountain rescue numbers in your phone for emergencies. In Ireland, call 999/112 and ask for mountain rescue. Remember: do not hesitate to call the emergency services as soon as you need them.
- Research your route in depth to establish if it's within your capabilities.
- Check opening/closing times of car parks if the start point is a public park, national park or privately owned park.
- Check weather forecasts to ensure you are dressed appropriately and pack the right gear, assess if it's safe to hike, or if you need to postpone.
- Check sunset times to ensure you leave with enough time to be back before dark.
- Check all your equipment is working and fully charged.
- Empty your car of valuables – remote car parks can be targets.
- Make sure you have enough fuel or car battery for your return journey.
- Inform a family member, friend or your place of residence of your hiking route and timings.
- Share your live location with a family member or WhatsApp group, so they can locate you if needed.
- Download the what3words app to get a precise location if needed in case of emergency.

During your hike

- Check for ticks, especially after passing overgrown areas.
- Don't share your hiking locations on social media to strangers until you are home.
- Place electronics and car keys in a waterproof case or dry bag.
- Know when to turn back. Sometimes we need to let go of ego and abandon a hike if the weather turns or we begin to feel unwell. The trails will be there for you another day.

Post hike

- Check yourself and your pets for ticks.
- Have snacks and extra hydration in the car to keep up energy levels if there's a long drive home.
- Change out of wet, cold clothes and boots and into fresh layers to help you reheat.

HIKING GEAR ESSENTIALS

BOOTS

There are many variables when choosing the best boots for you. It's worth going into a store to try them on; most adventure stores are fantastic and will be able to advise you based on your needs and budget. Boots should be comfortable, weatherproof and offer support and grip. Ensure you wear in new boots before hitting the trails – wear them around the house while they are nice and clean. If you opt for weatherproof boots, make sure you follow the care instructions when washing.

SOCKS

Good socks are just as important as boots. Good hiking socks will prevent rubbing and blisters.

RUCKSACK

Picking a suitable and comfortable rucksack is very important, particularly for longer hikes. Again, it is worth trying rucksacks in store, as different bags suit different body proportions. You want a rucksack that is lightweight, with strong and well-positioned straps to distribute the weight and ensure comfort. It is also advisable to get a waterproof cover for your rucksack if it doesn't come with one or ensure you pack using dry bags (see Hiking Kit Additional on p.11).

HEADWEAR

Depending on the conditions you will need a warm hat or cap/sun hat. In colder weather, a balaclava is a great way to keep both your head and neck warm. Buffs or snoods can also be adapted to be used as a hat or neck warmer. One of the easiest ways to warm up on a hike is to put on a hat. And vice versa, you can take it off to cool down.

GLOVES OR MITTENS	Opt for weatherproof gloves if you can. In colder conditions it's great to have two pairs – one lighter pair and an insulating thicker glove to go over them.
SUNGLASSES	You will often need these throughout the year, even in Ireland! Protecting your eyes is vital. Sport sunglasses are often the best for hiking.
BASE LAYER	Choose synthetic moisture-wicking material or wool. See page 6 for more detail on layering.
INSULATING LAYER	A fleece and/or insulating jacket.
WEATHERPROOF LAYER	Waterproof and windproof jacket and bottoms.
GAITERS (OPTIONAL)	Gaiters slip over your hiking boots and cover part of your legs. They are very beneficial in boggy or snowy conditions.

HIKING KIT ESSENTIALS

These are items that I bring with me to keep myself safe and ensure an enjoyable hike.

PHONE AND BATTERY PACK

Make sure your phone is fully charged. A battery pack is useful for longer hikes, especially if you are using apps and taking pictures.

FIRST AID

First-aid kits can be bought in most pharmacies and outdoor stores. A pocket first-aid kit is ideal for easier trails. A larger hiking-specific kit, which contain items for treating common hiking issues, is recommended for longer days on the trail. Some items you may want to add to a standard first-aid kit include: blister patches, heat patches, medication for pain/discomfort, any medical instructions you may want people to know, eye wash (something I have surprisingly used a lot!), tweezers or tick remover, hand sanitiser and SPF.

You should get into the habit of checking your first-aid kit regularly – refilling items and replacing anything out of date.

HEAD TORCH

Especially important for sunrise or sunset hikes, or if you get delayed on a hike. Ensure you check the charge before setting out.

SPF

Even on an overcast day, SPF is important. Ensure you opt for a sweatproof SPF; you don't want it running into your eyes mid-hike. Best kept in your first-aid kit, as you may need to reapply during your hike.

TICK REMOVER

Best kept in your first-aid kit.

WHISTLE

Comes with many hiking rucksacks, and is an important safety device if you get lost/injured.

NAVIGATION TOOLS

Having a map and compass, if you know how to use them, will ensure you are not caught out by a dead phone battery. If you are also using online maps make sure you download them before you leave for your hike as many hiking destinations have no phone coverage.

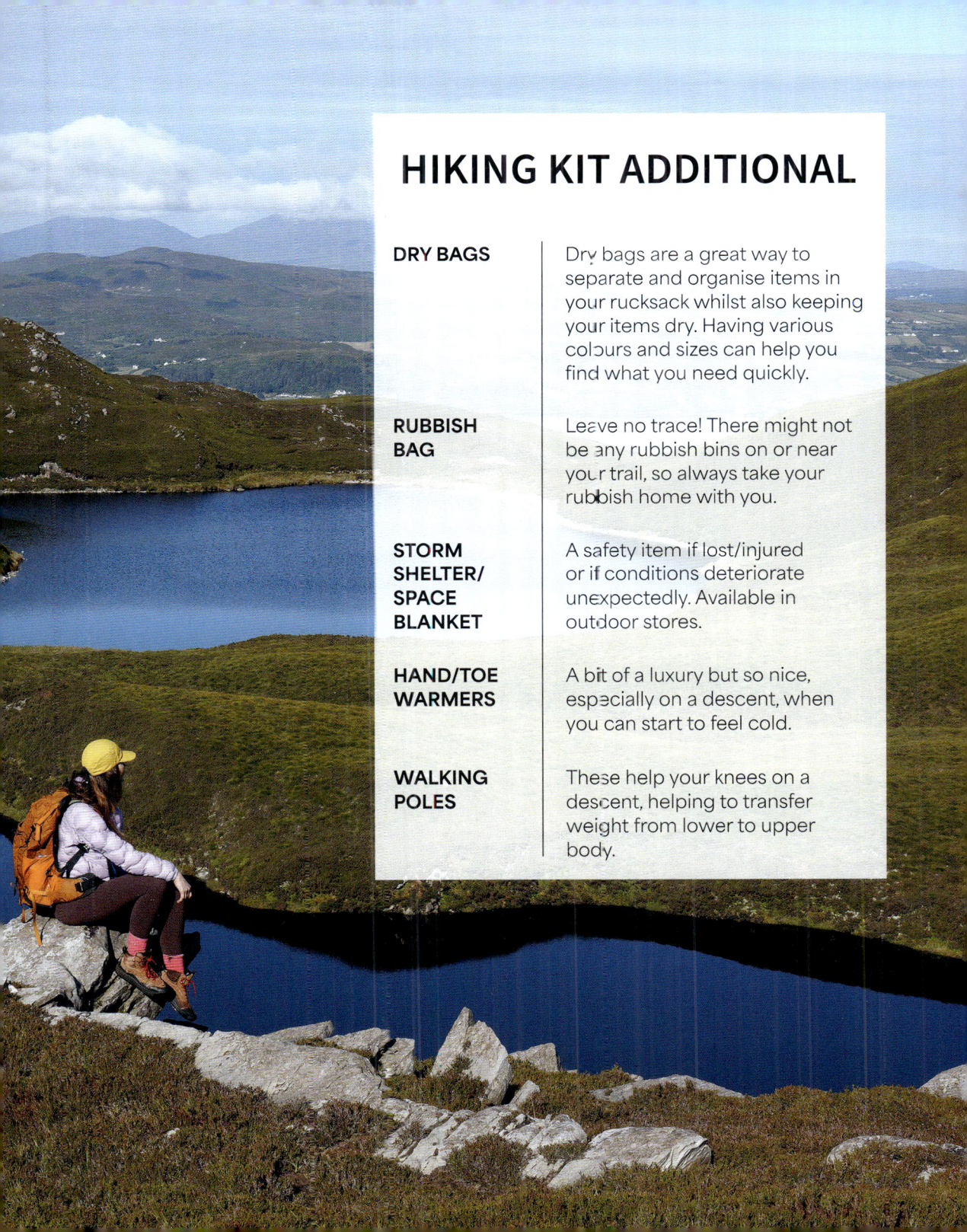

HIKING KIT ADDITIONAL

DRY BAGS	Dry bags are a great way to separate and organise items in your rucksack whilst also keeping your items dry. Having various colours and sizes can help you find what you need quickly.
RUBBISH BAG	Leave no trace! There might not be any rubbish bins on or near your trail, so always take your rubbish home with you.
STORM SHELTER/ SPACE BLANKET	A safety item if lost/injured or if conditions deteriorate unexpectedly. Available in outdoor stores.
HAND/TOE WARMERS	A bit of a luxury but so nice, especially on a descent, when you can start to feel cold.
WALKING POLES	These help your knees on a descent, helping to transfer weight from lower to upper body.

HIKING WITH YOUR DOG

As an animal lover, I often hike with my two dogs – Myla and Wilko. It is important to know that not all hikes in Ireland are dog friendly, and many cross privately owned land and farms. It is very important that you check in advance whether a hike is dog friendly or not, and keep your dog on a leash at all times to protect wildlife, livestock and of course your own dog from getting lost or injured. Maintaining access to the trails is important, and we all have our part to play in protecting the livelihoods of the people who live and farm in these areas, and who give us access. Dogs chasing livestock causes extreme stress to their animals, causing injury or death. Responsible dog ownership plays a vital role in maintaining permission to access the dog-friendly trails of Ireland.

Some items to bring with you include:

- Harness and lead
- Collapsible water bowl
- Water and treats, if required
- Reflector band/flashing light for harness
- Dry towel for afterwards
- Tick remover (you can use the one in your first-aid kit)
- Poo bags (and something to carry them in as there will be no bins)
- Jacket (some dogs may need one for the colder weather)

Always remember to leave no trace. You might think because you're out in nature it's okay to let your dog do its business and leave it, but this can be a danger to other animals, so always bring poo bags and dispose of your poo bags in a bin, not in nature – even the compostable ones!

WILDLIFE

What to do when you find an animal in need during your hike?

During your hike or while travelling to these destinations you may come across animals in need. I have come across plenty of wildlife and farm animals sick, or in danger, during my hikes so I wanted to share what resources there are to help.

1. Keep your distance. Take a photo or video using your zoom function on your camera, showcasing the condition of the animal as best you can. For example, bird covered in oil, seal stuck in plastic, pup abandoned or horse with a cut. Take zoomed out photos and videos to give an idea of the location of the animal.

2. Get a geotag or pin location for the area as close as possible to the animal.

3. Contact one of the rescue services or organisations as outlined here.

WILDLIFE
(deer, birds, foxes, hedgehogs etc.)

Kildare Wildlife Rescue – an amazing service with volunteers across the country. They have saved two birds I've found.

Email: info@kwr.ie

FARM ANIMALS
(when it is not a case of animal cruelty and you cannot locate an owner)

Department of Agriculture Animal Welfare (DAFM) – this offers a great service to get local vets out to the animal.

Email: animalwelfare@agriculture.gov.ie

Phone: 01 6072379 / 0761064408 / 1850211990

MARINE ANIMALS

Seal Rescue Ireland – once again, a fantastic service with volunteers nationwide.

Website: sealrescueireland.org

Rescue Hotline: 0871955393

For other marine wildlife strandings call ORCA's Marine Wildlife Stranding responders hotline: 0984625374.

IF YOU FIND A DOG WHILE HIKING

If you can safely secure the animal, check their collar for a tag.

If there is no collar with details, you could bring it to local vet to scan for a microchip.

Failing that, and if you are happy to take resposibility for the dog until finding the owner, you could try to use the power of social media to reunite the animal with its owner.

If you cannot find an owner, or do not feel safe approaching the dog, you can report to the ISPCA who can help further with next steps.

APPS AND WEBSITES

Weather

I use a few weather apps and websites depending where I am in the country. Some are more reliable than others depending on the location. I always check a few when researching and planning for a hike, to get the best picture I possibly can of weather conditions and how likely they are to change during my hike.

WINDY.COM	This is the app I use the most for checking weather. It is great for radar and satellite imagery. The different layers available to view are fantastic – especially the low, medium and high cloud layers.
YR.NO	Great for general hourly breakdowns in a specific area.
MOUNTAIN-FORECAST.COM	I love this to look at the weather on top of the mountain, e.g., windspeed at 700m up.
MET.IE	Met Eireann is the Irish Meteorological Service. It's great for keeping an eye on weather warnings and a good way to check rainfall with their live radar.
PHOTOPILLS	Perfect for planning a sunrise or sunset hike, and choosing the best location for both, depending on the time of year.

Tracking and Planning

STRAVA	Run, Bike, Hike
ALLTRAILS	Hike, Run, Walk
OUTDOORACTIVE	Online OSI/OSNI maps, route planning and tracking

GOOGLE MAPS	The start points and coordinates in this book are based on using Google Maps. The app is great to explore your favourite locations or if you come across a hidden waterfall or rock pool. The app's satellite layer is very handy for scouting car parks and layby areas in advance – use the image function to check for height barriers or other obstructions. It's my go-to app for finding hikes, eateries and scanning coastal areas for cool dipping spots.

Safety

WHAT3WORDS	Navigation and maps

Fun apps

Some apps are free, some are paid for and some have In-App purchases.

PICTURETHIS - PLANT IDENTIFIER	Allows you to scan plants and trees to learn all about them. On some phones this technology is now built into your camera. So do check to see if you have it.
MERLIN BIRD ID	Basically Shazam for birds, allowing you to learn about the birds whose songs you are hearing.
NIGHT SKY	Great for late night or early morning hikes to identify stars, constellations and more.
PEAK FINDER	Helps you to identify the mountains you are looking at in the distance.
IWDG	Marine wildlife has gained huge popularity in Ireland and in some ways goes hand-in-hand with hiking. Thanks to social media we've seen the like of mirke, humpback whales and basking sharks all exploring our shores. There have been many times on coastal routes I've seen pods of dolphins or basking sharks. This app allows you to see the most recent sightings which is handy if you're in the area and want to go have a look and it also allows you to log sightings you see. A great app for people wanting to get a glimpse of these magnificent creatures.

LEAVE NO TRACE

As you explore the outdoors you have a responsibility to leave the environment the same or better than you found it. Leave No Trace Ireland is an organisation which shows how we can protect the natural environment as we enjoy it. There are seven main principles to Leave No Trace, which are vital to be conscious of while adventuring. Below is a brief overview, but I would encourage everyone to learn about Leave No Trace at **leavenotraceireland.org**. They offer excellent training courses which are time well spent, or there's an introductory online course on their website which takes around 45 minutes to complete.

Plan Ahead and Prepare

Research the area you plan to adventure in, **know your route and be responsible for your safety** so you don't put yourself and others in danger. Respect closures and regulations.

Be Considerate of Others

The outdoor space is shared, so respect other hikers, the local landowners, their livelihoods and the community you are visiting. Simple things such as: stepping aside to let someone by, wearing earphones rather than carrying a speaker, parking appropriately and safely without blocking local access and gateways.

Respect Farm Animals and Wildlife

The majority of land we hike across is privately owned, so it's important we respect it as a place of work. Keep a distance from farm animals and wildlife, and **be a responsible dog owner**. Rural landowners play a huge role in allowing access for hillwalking.

Travel and Camp on Durable Ground

Stay on designated trails as much as possible. **Designated trails** protect the ground around them to allow the flora, fauna, rock and wildlife to remain undisturbed. Likewise, with camping, stick to established camping sites.

Leave What You Find

Always leave the outdoors as you find it. There's an array of historically and culturally significant structures on Irish hillwalking trails which should remain untouched.

Minimise the Effects of Fire

Fires can cause huge, irreversible and devastating damage to areas, so it's important to be informed and follow the advice from leavenotraceireland.org.

Dispose of Waste Properly

There are no bins on most trails. **Anything you bring with you, you take home**, and if you come across other people's rubbish, bring that home too! Avoiding polluting water sources and dispose of human waste appropriately.

TICKS

Ticks are very prevalent in Ireland. I have already mentioned carrying tick removers, and checking yourself and your pets post-hike (see page 7), what else can we know and do to protect ourselves and pets?

What are ticks?

Ticks are spider-like creatures. They come in a few different shapes and sizes but commonly they all feed on the blood of humans and animals.

When and where can you find them?

They are most active between spring and autumn. Ticks can be found in the outdoors in both rural areas, like mountains, woodland, parks, and urban areas across Ireland.

What can they do?

Ticks can carry infections, like Lyme disease and more.

What simple ways are there to prevent tick bites?

There are topical treatments or tablets for pets that can provide protection for weeks or months depending on what brand you opt for. It's still essential to check pets after hiking, even when using these treatments, as your pets can simply carry them into your home or car and pass them onto you or other people.

What can people do?

- **Clothing: Wear long pants and tops,** pull socks over loose trouser ends. Light colours will help you spot them. Tie back hair or wear a hat. **Tip:** I carry a lint roller to go over my clothes before getting back into my car as an extra help in searching for these bugs.

- Use **a repellent** on skin and clothes.

- Stick to trails and worn tracks, **avoiding overgrown areas** where possible, which is sometimes hard in Ireland.

- **Check yourself and pets** well, especially in the key areas such as your warm skin folds: underarms, behind knees and scalp and so on.

It's important to do this as soon as you reach your car and even during hike breaks. The HSE.ie states Lyme disease from a tick bite can be prevented if the tick is removed within 24 to 36 hours; this is why checking and getting them removed quickly is so important.

After checking yourself, check your outdoor gear like your backpack and the hood of your jacket for ticks. Wash clothes rather than leaving them lying around and bringing ticks into your bedroom or bathroom. Shower as soon as you can once home, so you can give yourself another thorough check.

What if you find a tick attached?

Depending on how long the tick has been attached, different recommendations and protocols are advised. Check out **ticktalk.org** and **HSE.ie** for up-to-date information, as you may need to visit your GP for medication.

Remove ticks carefully and correctly. You need to remove the entire tick, making sure it does not break off in part, using a tick remover or tweezer. See **ticktalk.org** for a step-by-step of this process, as it is crucial to perform this correctly.

Then wash the area with soap and water. Next, keep an eye out for symptoms, such as a rash in the area, or fever within several weeks and seek medical advice immediately if symptoms occur.

See **HSE.ie** for full symptom list and latest advice to ensure you manage a bite correctly and get appropriate treatment.

TERMINOLOGY

In this book, summary statistics are included at the beginning of each of the fifty hikes. This is a good way to compare the different hikes and get an overview of what to expect. The summary statistics are explained here:

OSI/OSNI	This is the relevant Ordnance Survey map number.
HEIGHT	Height is in metres, and refers to the peak's height above sea level.
DISTANCE	Distance is indicated in kilometres (km) for the trail as described. This may be more or less if you veer off the trail.
APPROX. TIME	The approximate time for the completion of the trail is based on a relatively good walking pace and includes time for short breaks.
DIFFICULTY	The hikes in this book are classified as easy, moderate, hard or very hard, as determined by terrain, elevation, distance, presence or not of waymarks, and the level of skill required.
ROUTE TYPE	This refers to the description of the route. There are four route types in this book: out-and-back, looped, A-to-B, or lollipop circuit.
STARTING POINT	The starting point refers to the nearest parking place to the trailhead.
ELEVATION	Elevation is in metres, and refers to the elevation gain from the starting point of your trail.
PARKING	A description of the car parking options near the trailhead.
PARKING FEE	Indication of whether there is a car parking charge. For some of the hikes this is cash only.
DOG-FRIENDLY	Indicates if a trail is dog friendly. All of the dog-friendly hikes in this book require that dogs are kept on a leash at all times.
PIT STOP	Showcases somewhere near the hike that is worth visiting – somewhere nice to eat, to take a picture, or to make some memories.

DIFFICULTY LEVELS

Check the difficulty rating of a route before you tackle it and ensure that you adequately prepare for your hike (page 5). There are four difficulty levels in this book: easy, moderate, hard and very hard. Some hikes may be classified across two difficulty levels; for example, moderate-hard.

These ratings relate to good weather conditions. Some hikes that are marked moderate may be very difficult in poor visibility and high winds, so remember to account for the weather and how that will impact each hike's rating.

Make sure you set yourself up for a successful adventure, and your hike will be a lot more fun.

Easy

Suitable for beginners, such as people who regularly walk in their day-to-day life and are ready to tackle uneven terrains, elevation and new surroundings. These hikes are typically well-marked or have identifiable trails along the likes of forest trails, grassy paths and surfaced roads with some moderate ascents. The walks may also be reasonably short.

Easy

Erris Head Loop	p.59
Union Rock	p.63
Devil's Chimney Waterfall	p.67
Cruagh Wood	p.89
Devil's Glen	p.97
Raven Wood Nature Reserve	p.131
Portrane to Donabate Coastal Walk	p.135
Three Castle Head	p.183
Ardmore Cliff Walk	p.193
Kilkee Cliff Walk and Loop Head	p.209
Tollymore Forest	p.253

Easy to Moderate

Mullaghgarve Mass Rock	p.77
Mullaghmeen	p.139
Abbey Hill	p.215
Horn Head	p.233
Fair Head	p.243

Moderate

Suitable for those who have hiking experience and have completed a range of beginner hikes with ease. These trails require some navigation and a good level of fitness; they will be steeper, longer and/or a little more exposed to the elements. Any difficult sections will be highlighted in the hike description. These trails are great to build up your stamina for a harder hike and to gain experience with different types of terrain.

Moderate

Tully Mountain	p.33
Mount Gable	p.47
Wild Nephin National Park	p.55
Bray Head and Hill	p.83
Scarr Mountain	p.93
Luggala Mountain	p.101
Sorrel Hill	p.115
Glen Beach Cliff Walk	p.121
Mount Leinster and Slieve Bawn	p.125
Cruach Mhárthain	p.145
Strickeen Mountain from Gap of Dunloe	p.155
Derrycunnihy Church to Lord Brandon's Cottage Mass Path	p.161
Bray Head, Valentia	p.165
Knockomagh	p.187
The Devil's Bit	p.201
Moylussa	p.205
Hen Mountain	p.259
Slieve Martin and Kodak Corner	p.265
Slieve Gullion	p.271

Moderate to Hard

Derrybawn Mountain	p.105
Turlough Hill, Camaderry and St Kevin's Way Loop	p.111
Gleninchaquin Park	p.173
Nire Valley Trails	p.197
Urris Lakes Loop	p.221

Hard

These hikes require high levels of fitness and previous hillwalking experience is essential; make sure you have completed a wide range of moderate hikes with confidence before attempting hard ones. Often these trails have a mix of terrain, including uneven and difficult ground like scree, narrow ridges, cliffs and steep ground over long sections. While some trails may be marked, sections or entire routes may require some navigation skills. See the list of Hiking Gear Essentials (page 10) to help you prepare for these hard hikes.

Very Hard

These hikes should only be attempted once you've mastered the hard hikes.

These are hikes which require very high levels of fitness and stamina, and a lot of hiking experience. These routes typically have difficult, rough terrain, prolonged steep climbs, and predominantly will have no marked or visible trail the entire route. These hikes will require solid navigation skills, specific hiking gear and mountain skills such as scrambling. These trails can be very remote, very dangerous and have very little footfall.

Hard			
Slievemore	p.51	Ben Crom	p.249
Benbulbin	p.71	**Very hard**	
Sauce Creek	p.149		
Knocknadobar	p.169	Benlettery	p.37
Knockalla Ridge	p.227	Benbaun	p.43
An Port to Glenlough Bay	p.237	Hungry Hill	p.177

Mountain Leaders and Mountain Skills

I recommend booking a mountain leader for hikes marked as hard or very hard. This is an enjoyable way to experience these routes while also learning about the area.

If you want to build up your hiking capabilities and confidence, I would also recommend taking a two-day mountain skills course where you can learn about navigation skills, route planning and mountain hazards, as well as personal equipment and much more. I credit these courses with helping me gain so much confidence in the outdoors. To find a course provider near you, check mountaineering.ie.

HIKING LIST

CONNACHT
- ☐ Tully Mountain
- ☐ Benlettery
- ☐ Benbaun
- ☐ Mount Gable
- ☐ Slievemore
- ☐ Wild Nephin National Park
- ☐ Erris Head Loop
- ☐ Union Rock
- ☐ Devil's Chimney Waterfall
- ☐ Benbulbin
- ☐ Mullaghgarve Mass Rock

LEINSTER
- ☐ Bray Head and Hill
- ☐ Cruagh Wood
- ☐ Scarr Mountain
- ☐ Devil's Glen
- ☐ Luggala Mountain
- ☐ Derrybawn Mountain
- ☐ Turlough Hill, Camaderry and St Kevin's Way Loop
- ☐ Sorrel Hill
- ☐ Glen Beach Cliff Walk
- ☐ Mount Leinster and Slieve Bawn
- ☐ Raven Woods Nature Reserve
- ☐ Portrane to Donabate Coastal Walk
- ☐ Mullaghmeen

MUNSTER
- ☐ Cruach Mhárthain
- ☐ Sauce Creek
- ☐ Strickeen Mountain from Gap of Dunloe
- ☐ Derrycunnihy Church to Lord Brandon's Cottage Mass Path
- ☐ Bray Head, Valentia
- ☐ Knocknadobar
- ☐ Gleninchaquin Park
- ☐ Hungry Hill
- ☐ Three Castle Head
- ☐ Knockomagh
- ☐ Ardmore Cliff Walk
- ☐ Nire Valley Trails
- ☐ The Devil's Bit
- ☐ Moylussa
- ☐ Kilkee Cliff Walk and Loop Head
- ☐ Abbey Hill

ULSTER
- ☐ Urris Lakes Loop
- ☐ Knockalla Ridge
- ☐ Horn Head
- ☐ An Port to Glenlough Bay
- ☐ Fair Head
- ☐ Ben Crom
- ☐ Tollymore Forest
- ☐ Hen Mountain
- ☐ Slieve Martin and Kodak Corner
- ☐ Slieve Gullion

Tully Mountain

Ir. Cnoc Leitreach, 'hill of the wet slope'

What You Need to Know

OSI: 37
Height: 356m
Distance: 5km
Approx. time: 1.5-2 hours
Difficulty: moderate
Route type: out-and-back
Starting point: Harbour Derryherbert
Elevation: 350m
Parking: yes, 2-3 cars
Fee: no
Dog friendly: yes, on a leash

Note: Harbour Derryherbert is a tiny layby area for 2 to 3 cars. It is very important to not block the pier access or gateways. Given this very limited parking, off-peak is the only time to enjoy this hike.

Tully Mountain, known locally as Letter Hill, holds a commanding position on the Renvyle Peninsula in Connemara. The summit of Tully Mountain offers expansive views of the Twelve Bens, as well as several islands off the west coast, including Inishbofin, Inishark, Crump Island and Clare Island. Some of Ireland's most spectacular beaches can also be viewed, and easily visited, from Tully. Among them, Glassilaun Beach, known for its white sands and crystal-clear blue waters. Glassilaun Beach is located at the mouth of Killary Fjord, one of Ireland's three glacial fjords. Of historical interest are the ruins of the pirate queen, Grace O'Malley's (Gráinne Mhaol) castle, on the western side of the peninsula.

This hike is a really nice alternative to the popular Diamond Hill; however, it's one to do at off-peak days and times due to the limited parking. For years, visiting Connemara while driving into Letterfrack from Moyard I would look across the water and think, *what is that hill?* A similar shape to Diamond Hill right along the coast, I knew the views would be amazing from the summit. Back in 2020 I finally got to give it a go for the first time and it did not disappoint. I really hope you love the views from this hike as much as I do.

Note: While the trail has become significantly more visible in the past few years, navigation tools and online tracking maps downloaded in advance will be useful.

PIT STOPS

Swim
- Glassilaun Beach
- Renvyle Beach

Visit
- Killary Fjord
- Kylemore Abbey
- Cleggan Cliffs
- Walled Victorian Garden

Eat
- Misunderstood Heron
- Sweet Nothings
- Kabo Coffee

THE TRAIL

From the pier, walk up the road towards Tully Mountain (leaving the pier and going left along the road); be aware of vehicles.

At approx. 370m, turn right along a lane that leads upwards. At 600m pass through a metal farm gate, making sure you close it behind you.

From here there is a narrow and worn trail. This is the rocky and boggy terrain that will lead you towards the summit.

Note: You just need to keep an eye out for the trail, and make sure you don't wander off course.

At approx. 1.9km you'll have a clear eyeline for the summit marker. Just before the summit at approx. 2.3km you get some really nice viewpoints (in my opinion, some of these are better than the summit).

From here, keep following the trail and at approx. 2.5km you will reach the summit marker.

Enjoy the views from the summit over Achill Sound, Bellmullet, Mweelrea Mountain, Croagh Patrick, Twelve Bens, Diamond Hill and south towards Cleggan.

Return the way you came.

Other Hikes in the Area

Benbaun (p.43)
Benlettery (p.37)

INCLUDED IN THE HIKE LIFE (BOOK ONE)

Ben Creggan (p.55)
Diamond Hill (p.59)
Mweelrea (p.49)
Errisbeg (p.69)

MORE TO EXPLORE

Omey Island Loop (7km)
Killary Harbour Coastal Walk (16km)

Benlettery

Ir. Binn Leitrí, 'peak of the wet hillsides'

Benlettery is within the Twelve Bens mountain range, and its most southerly peak. If you are looking for a challenging but relatively short climb in the Twelve Bens, this is it. The climb and the summit offer remarkable views across the Connemara landscape and beyond, so it is worth taking as many breaks as you can to enjoy them.

As the translation of its name suggests, Benlettery can be wet and boggy. Local legend has it that, at some times of the year, there is a pool of water at the summit that turns your hair white if you wash in it. You have been warned!

Benlettery offers a magnificent backdrop to Ballynahinch Castle and lake. Although the former is now a luxury hotel, it was once the home of Richard Martin, also known as Humanity Dick, an Irish politician and the founder of the Society for the Prevention of Cruelty to Animals in 1822.

I really enjoy Benlettery, as I love a steep climb and appreciate the mix of terrain, especially some scrambling. It is also a great opportunity to use navigation skills, all of which make hiking Benlettery

What You Need to Know

OSI: 44
Height: 577m
Distance: 4.4km
Approx. time: 2.5-3 hours
Difficulty: very hard
Route type: out-and-back
Starting point: Ben Lettery Connemara Hostel
Elevation: 557m
Parking: yes, 3-4 spaces outside Ben Lettery Hostel
Fee: no
Dog friendly: no

Recommended mountain leader:
Ger; climbconnemara@gmail.com
Michelle; wildfullstop.com

feel like a real adventure. It is very tough physically, but short, and the spectacular views make it well worth the effort.

Note: There are no markings for this trail. However, there are sections where you will see evidence of footfall and a vague trail. I recommend using navigation, both OSI maps and online route planners, to help track your route. This is also an extremely steep trail and walking poles are recommended, especially for the steep descent. I recommend only doing this hike on a clear day, as having the summit in sight is useful. My approx. distance references below are for a direct route to the summit. Every time I do this trail the distances change, depending on how much I zigzag. It is usually anything between 2 and 2.3km to reach the summit.

Other Hikes in the Area

Benbaun (p.43)
Tully Mountain (p.33)

INCLUDED IN *THE HIKE LIFE* (BOOK ONE)
Diamond Hill (p.59)

MORE TO EXPLORE
Benlettery and Bengower Loop (a continuation of this hike, looped and longer in distance, approx. 6.9km), this would need OSI maps 44 /37.

Glencoaghan Loop (continuation of this hike that goes on to cover 17km crossing Bengower, Benbreen, Bencollaghduff, Bencorr and Derryclare, one of the best horseshoe trails in Connemara, for which a mountain leader is recommended).

THE TRAIL

Starting at the roadside, walk in towards the hostel. As you approach the building, to your left you will see a stile. Cross over the stile heading right to begin the immediate sharp ascent.

This section is a grassy slope through some trees. At approx. 400m you will cross over a fence. Find a section of fence which is suitable to do so.

From here you are on the open mountain, and there is no trail aside from a vague track in a few sections. It

is an extremely steep grassy and rocky ascent.

> **Note:** I find that the route along here offers some incredible views, so take breaks and enjoy the views back over Ballynahinch Lake.

At approx. 1.3km you will reach a small rock pile and the shoulder of Benlettery; this section gives such superb views – be sure to stop to take them in.

From here the climb gets rockier, with the odd section of bog, and as you climb higher there are sections of loose rock with some scrambling sections over large rocks.

At approx. 2km you will reach the summit of Benlettery, marked by a large pile of rocks. There are amazing views here of Glynsk Lough and Ballinafad Lough.

You can walk along the summit, and at approx. 100m there is a small plateau that offers incredible vistas out to the north over the peaks of Connemara National Park and east across to the Glencoaghan Valley.

Return the way you came. Take good care on the steep descent.

PIT STOPS

Swim
- Coral Strand, Mannin Bay
- Dog's Bay (off-peak times are best)

Visit
- Pine Island Viewpoint
- Cleggan Cliffs
- Lough Inagh ViewPoint
- Drive Sky Road

Eat
- Ballynahinch Castle

In Clifden
- Steam Café
- Guys Bar Clifden
- The Lamplight
- The Willow Tree Restaurant
- Mitchell's Restaurant
- Upstairs Downstairs Café

In Ballyconneely
- Sweet Nothings

In Roundstone
- Coffee Cottage
- O'Dowd's Seafood Bar & Restaurant
- The Bogbean Café

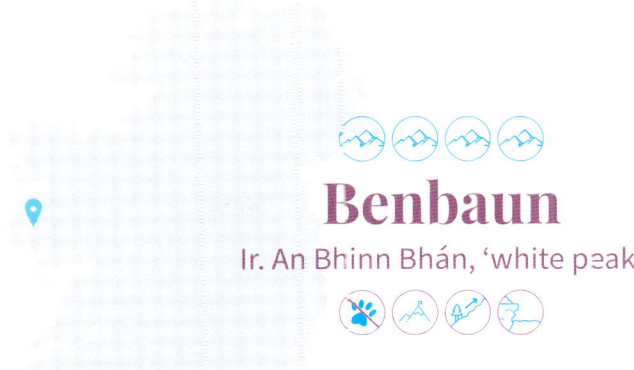

Benbaun

Ir. An Bhinn Bhán, 'white peak'

Benbaun is Galway's highest peak, and it's also the highest point of the Twelve Bens range in Connemara. So, as you can probably guess, it is a beast of a climb, one to put on your list if you are an experienced hiker. It is not advised to climb this in poor weather, or if you do not have the necessary skills and tools to navigate.

Benbaun, or the 'White Mountain', gets its name from the distinctive white quartz rock found in the area. Interestingly, the name Twelve Bens is a bit of a misnomer as there are actually at least 20 peaks in the Connemara range, and no one knows which 12 are being referred to. In Irish the range is simply known as *na BeannaBeola*, 'the peaks of Beola', with no mention of a number. The Beola in question was a giant and Chieftain of the Fír Bolg, the fourth settlers of Ireland in Irish mythology.

Benbaun is also part of the Glencorbet Horseshoe Loop, a 14km trail covering Benfree, Benbrack, Benbaun and Loughmore. This is a very challenging hike and I recommend that you book a mountain leader for it (see hike details).

What You Need to Know

OSI: 37
Height: 729m
Distance: 9.6km
Approx. time: 3.5-4 hours
Difficulty: very hard, only for experienced hikers
Route type: out-and-back
Starting point: Benbaun Trailhead car park
Elevation: 700m
Parking: 4-5 spaces
Fee: no
Dog friendly: no

Recommended mountain leader:
Ger; climbconnemara@gmail.com
Michelle; wildfullstop.com

Note: This route is for experienced hikers who have necessary navigation skills and are familiar with steep and dangerous terrain.

The trail description below is a general overview of the route: it does not replace the navigation tools required.

Other Hikes in the Area

Benlettery (p.37)
Tully Mountain (p.33)

INCLUDED IN *THE HIKE LIFE* (BOOK ONE)
Diamond Hill (p.59)

MORE TO EXPLORE
Glencorbet Horseshoe Loop (14km)

THE TRAIL

Note: Avoid after heavy or consistent rainfall as there are some river and stream crossings, and the route can become very boggy.

From the small car park area at Benbaun Trailhead, follow the mountain roadway, a minor gravel road with a grassy middle section.

At approx. 1.5km the roadway will meet a river; the river may be difficult to cross depending on the time of year and any recent rainfall. There are large stones to help you across.

After crossing the river, continue on following the roadway.

At approx. 1.7km the trail splits, left up to a building and right onto a grassy wide path: keep right.

Now this is where many go wrong! At approx. 1.9km, just before you meet the roadway again, turn right, passing by the walls of an old stone building. Here the trail runs between two fences before coming down to run adjacent to the river.

The fence will be to your left-hand side.

At approx. 2.2km, the fence ends; at this point, veer left to begin your ascent up along the steep grassy slope. There will be a stream to your right-hand side.

The route now follows a stream upwards.

At approx. 3.2km the route meanders across the stream, where it continues along a worn trail, the stream is now on your left-hand side.

At approx. 3.7km you will be on the shoulder of Benbaun, and from here the trail gets very rocky.

As you ascend further, there is loose rock and, in some sections, a worn trail. You will see that this section is marked by two cairns.

At approx. 4.7km you reach the summit marker. You are now at the highest point in Connemara! Enjoy this amazing vantage point across the peaks of the region, and beyond, on a clear day.

PIT STOPS

Swim
- Glassilaun Beach
- Renvyle Beach

Visit
- Kylemore Abbey
- Killary Harbour (for the views)
- Aasleagh Falls
- Lough Nafooey Waterfall (be warned it is a bit of an adventure to get there!)

Eat
- Kabo Coffee
- Misunderstood Heron
- The Purple Door Café
- Hamilton's Bar & Restaurant

Mount Gable

Ir. Binn Shleibhe, 'peak of the mountain/moorland'

What You Need to Know

OSI: 38
Height: 417.8m
Distance: 6.4km
Approx. time: 2 hours
Difficulty: moderate
Route type: out-and-back, looped option available
Starting point: Mount Gable car park, Gortnarup, Galway
Elevation: 280m
Parking: yes, about 10 spaces
Fee: no
Dog friendly: yes, on a leash

PIT STOPS

Swim
- Touramkeady Waterfall (pictured)

Visit
- Lough Nafooey Waterfall (it's an adventure and walk to get there)
- Hill of Doon Viewing
- Castlekirk
- Cong Abbey
- Kelly's Cave, Cong
- Ard Na Gaoithe, Forest Recreational Park
- Lough Mask - Tourmakeady Pier
- Glengowla Mines

Eat
- Keane's Bar, Maam Bridge
- Cullen's at the Cottage
- Pat Cohan's Gastro Pub - The Quiet Man Bar
- My Little Flower Coffee
- Powers Thatch Bar & Restaurant
- Connemara Greenway Restaurant
- Sullivan's Country Grocer
- Brigit's Garden & Café

This trail follows the *Seanbhóthar*, or 'Old Road' between the Corr na Móna and An Fhairche villages. You will come across several ruins along the trail, including the remains of a typical famine-era village on the lakes of Lough Coolin, with the cottages clustered closely together to provide protection from the elements. There are also wonderful views of Lough Corrib to the lower side of the road.

Lough Corrib is the second largest lake on the island of Ireland. There have been a considerable number of archaeological finds in the lake, including canoes from the Bronze Age and Iron Age.

> **Note:** This trail is not waymarked. Navigation tools are necessary to help guide you, particularly on the summit plateau.

There is also a loop option available for this trail that brings you down via Lough Coolin, which is approx. 2km extra with a section of road.

THE TRAIL

From the car park, cross over the stile. From here there is a well-worn, rocky and grassy trail which gradually rises. In some sections the trail becomes narrow and grassy but remains distinctive.

At approx. 1.2km you will reach the long plateau of Mount Gable.

The trail will veer left leading towards a small rock pile which you will reach at approx. 1.5km.

The trail from here is less obvious, as you traverse across to the summit marker. The ground here is undulating, passing by some small rock piles and large sections of eroded bog.

At approx. 3km you will reach the summit marker where you can enjoy amazing views over towards Connemara National Park, Lough Corrib and Bohaun, Knocknagussy and Lugnbrick mountains.

Take time to explore the large summit area and take in the views.

I like to walk east approx. 200m from the summit, where there is another cairn with views down over Lough Coolin and the impressive Lough Mask.

Return the way you came.

Slievemore

Achill

Ir. An Sliabh Mór [GÉ], 'the big mountain'

On the southern slopes of Slievemore mountain, you will see the ruins of Slievemore Village. There are somewhere between 80 and 100 cottage ruins. The village was originally abandoned during the Great Hunger of 1845 to 1852, owing to rent increases and emigration. The cottages were then in use as 'booleys' or summer houses until the 1940s. The practice of 'booleying' involved moving location based on the seasons and the availability of grass for livestock. During the summer months it is possible to book a tour of The Deserted Village with a local guide. The Oscar-winning film The Banshees of Inisherin was filmed on location on Achill Island and on Inishmore, one of the Aran Islands. Achill Tourism has produced a 'Banshees of Inisherin' trail map that takes you to some of the film's most recognisable locations, including Keem Bay, home to one of Ireland's most magnificent beaches.

There are two main routes up Slievemore, from the west Deserted Village or from east Dugort Beach; the most direct is from Dugort as described below. However, you could enjoy the best of both and do the loop trail - this is 12km and has

What You Need to Know

OSI: 22/30
Height: 671m
Distance: 4.8km
Approx. time: 2.5-3 hours
Difficulty: hard
Route type: out-and-back
Starting point: Strand Hotel, Dugort
Elevation: 660m
Parking: yes, parking at the beach and near the Strand Hotel
Fee: no
Dog friendly: no

Recommended mountain leader:
Allan Mcgee; allanmcgee509@hotmail.com

a section on the road. Slievemore appears intimidating when looking up from sea level; its sharp ridge and towering outline often cast a shadow over Dugort beach below. It looks impressive, though, so make sure you get a photo of yourself looking up at Slievemore from the beach!

Slievemore's location right on the sea means bad weather can roll in very fast. So, even though this hike is short, it's extremely steep and has exposed cliff drops, which means that navigation experience and appropriate gear are essential.

Note: This trail is best avoided after rainfall as it can be very slippery. Avoid in bad weather. The below is just a general over view of the route make sure to have navigational tools.

THE TRAIL

From the car park, walk up the road towards Dugort Pier. Take the first road left, and almost immediately you'll see a narrow trail to your right which runs up beside a shed.

This is the trail start. It is a narrow grassy trail which turns into a distinctive rocky trail leading quickly up onto the open mountain.

The route runs directly upward along Slievemore's shoulder. It runs adjacent to the shoulder's steep cliffs to your right-hand side, not directly along them. Keep a safe distance from the edge.

This section is an extremely steep uphill gradient.

The higher you go, the rockier the trail

PIT STOPS

Places are often seasonal here so check before you go!

Swim
- Keem Bay
- Dugort Beach

Visit
- The Deserted Village
- Sabhna Saunsa, Dugort Beach
- The White Cliffs of Ashleam
- Minaun Heights
- Seven-Circuit Classical Labyrinth
- Keel Beach (for a stroll)
- Lynott's Pub
- Pure Magic (for watersports)

Eat
- Achill Island Kitchen @ Dooagh Shop
- Bervie Guesthouse
- Blásta at Ted's
- Lílí Bán (for coffee)
- The Amethyst Bar
- Beehive Crafts and Gifts
- Nadurtha Soul Food Bar & Café

See Wild Nephin Natioanl Park (p.55) for more reccomendations.

becomes; you will have to use your hands to hoist yourself up over the rocks.

At approx. 2.1km you'll get your first view of the summit. Here the trail levels out, crossing over some eroded bog on to a grassy trail towards the summit.

At approx. 2.4km you'll come to the large cairn; and behind it is the summit marker.

This hike is an out-and-back trail, so you can return the way you came, being careful on the descent.

Other Hikes in the Area

Wild Nephin National Park (p.55)

INCLUDED IN *THE HIKE LIFE* **(BOOK ONE)**
Croaghaun (p.41)

MORE TO EXPLORE
Claggan Mountain Broadwalk (2km)

Wild Nephin National Park

Ir: Néifinn Fhiáin [OSI]. 'sanctuary'

The Wild Nephin National Park covers 15,000 hectares of land with the Nephin Beg Mountain range at its centre and is Ireland's first designated wilderness area. The Wild Nephin National Park is also an International Dark Sky Park, where you can experience the visual wonder of the solar system without light pollution. Creating the Park involved over a decade of re-wilding activity, including the remaking of forest roads into walking trails, and the creation of huts for wild camping. The Park is also home to Owenduff Bog, the largest expanse of intact Atlantic blanket bog in Ireland and western Europe.

This National Park is a complete dream for hikers; it's very well maintained, organised and, on most occasions, quiet. A question I always ask experienced hikers when I meet them is, 'What is your favourite hidden gem hike?' and about half of them give the answer, 'A hike in the Wild Nephin National Park.'

You can also camp here at the designated camp zones, which is a brilliant way to fully experience the night sky after a day of hiking. To do this, you will need to

What You Need to Know

OSI: 23/31
Distance: 5km
Approx. time: 1-1.5 hours
Difficulty: moderate (due to terrain)
Route type: looped
Starting point: Letterkeen Trailhead
Elevation: 85m
Parking: yes, about 18-20 spaces
Fee: no
Dog friendly: yes, on a leash

Other Hikes in the Area

Slievemore (p.51)
Erris Head Loop (p.59)

INCLUDED IN *THE HIKE LIFE* (BOOK ONE)
Nephin (p.37)
Croaghaun (p.41)
Croagh Patrick (p.45)

PIT STOPS

Swim
- Mulranny Beach

Visit
- Ballycroy Visitor Centre (amazing and helpful staff there)
- Old Irish Goat Centre (a must!)
- Nephin Drive (coming from Keenagh crossroad is incredible)
- Claggan Mountain Costal Trail
- Mulranny Causeway
- Mulranny Machiar Dunes
- Greenway Lane (art studio-café)

Eat
- Ginger & Wild Café, Ballycroy Visitor Centre
- Nevin's Newfield Inn
- Kelly's Kitchen, Newport

See Slievemore (p.51) for more recommendation around Achill.

get a permit via campingwildnephin.com. The Park also asks hikers to register on their online system in case of emergency.

There are so many hikes and trails here: whether you're a beginner or an experienced hiker, you are guaranteed to enjoy this park. Here are some of the options:

- Varys Loop (easy, 2.5km, orange)
- Bothy Loop (moderate, 5km, blue)
- Lough Aroher Loop (hard, 10km, red)
- Letterkenn Loop (hard, 12km, purple)
- Bangor trail (40km)
- Western Way (200km)
- Nephin Beg (16.5km, no markers)
- Slieve Carr & Corslieve (10km, no markers)
- Glendahurk Horeshoe, which includes Corranbinnia (16km, no markers)

Note: Go to the Wild Nephin National Park Lookout. Here you'll get the best view of all the peaks – and it's particularly amazing at sunrise or sunset!

THE TRAIL

The trail I'm describing here is the Bothy Loop. It is well marked and suitable for most hikers on their trip to Nephin – as long as they're okay with very uneven, mixed terrain.

> **Note:** You will be looking out for the blue arrow waymarkers, which are very clear throughout.

At the car park, take a photo of the information board in case you need it.

Follow the blue arrow down a narrow gravel trail that crosses over a wooden bridge. (This is a great photo spot).

From here, the trail turns grassy, boggy and rocky and runs alongside the river, which will be to your left-hand side. At approx. 360m you cross over a metal stile.

The trail continues to run alongside the river; it will get rockier in some sections and please be aware that it can get very boggy after rain or flooding.

At approx. 1.1km you'll cross over the river on a metal bridge, in the shape of a triangle, this can be slippery! (This is a great photo spot).

The trail continues on a narrow track and at approx. 1.4km it passes over another stile, onto a boardwalk for a short section and then it crosses another wooden bridge. (This is a great photo spot).

From here, the trail is a narrow grassy track. At approx. 1.8km you pass through a small metal gate onto a fire road and the

route turns right. From here, you follow this rocky fire road. At approx. 4km it goes over a stone bridge and continues back towards the car park, then at approx. 5km you'll reach a barrier leading into the car park itself.

Erris Head Loop

Ir. Ceann Iorrais, 'headland of the peninsula'

Erris Head is a Special Area of Conservation due to its rich biodiversity. On the trail you are likely to see a variety of sea birds, including fulmars, falcons, gulls and Barnacle geese. Also keep an eye out for hares and frogs on land, and dolphins and seals in the Atlantic Ocean. From the trail you can see Eagle Rock and its lighthouse. The lighthouse and keepers cottage were commissioned in 1830, to help boats navigate the many islands and stacks in this part of the ocean. Lighthouse keepers served on Eagle Rock until 1988. The lighthouse was electrified in 1968 and adapted to solar power in 2001. There are also numerous islands and stacks viewable from the trail, including Illandavuck Island, Pigeon Rock and the Stags of Broadhaven. There is also a Second World War, ÉIRE navigational sign on the hillside of Erris Head; there are more than 80 of these huge whitewashed landmarks around the Irish coast

The trail is also close to Blacksod, an area with lots to see and do, and a surprising link to D-Day! On 6 June 1944, Allied Forces landed on the beaches of Normandy, initiating the end of the Second World War. However, D-Day was originally scheduled for 5 June, but was

What You Need to Know

OSI: 22
Distance: 5.3km
Approx. time: 1.5-2 hours
Difficulty: easy
Route type: looped
Starting point: Erris Head Loop Walk, Glenara Belmullet, Mayo
Elevation: 140m
Parking: yes, about 15-20 spaces
Fee: no
Dog friendly: no

Other Hikes in the Area

INCLUDED IN *THE HIKE LIFE* **(BOOK ONE)**
Benwee Head Cliff Walk (p.33)

postponed due to an adverse weather report from Blacksod Lighthouse, made by then 21-year-old Maureen Sweeney. Many historians assert that bad weather on the original date would have negatively impacted the Allied forces' chances of success.

Erris Head Loop is close to Belmullet, one of my favourite places in Ireland. I particularly love the incredible tidal pool there, which is a must see after this hike. I love the rugged coastline and remarkable history and stories of the area as well. The pit stops I have listed below are really worth going to, especially if you like myths and legends.

THE TRAIL

The trail is marked with purple arrows and some sections of the trail are worn, while others are not. However, the markers make this hike easy to follow in good weather conditions. But it would not be suitable in high winds or low visibility.

At the car park there is an information board about the trail which is worth taking a photo of.

From the car park, cross over the green stile. Follow the worn trail as it runs along by the fence, which is to your right-hand side.

At approx. 300m you'll cross over another stile.

Again, at approx. 460m, you'll cross over another stile. Immediately turn left,

PIT STOPS

Swim
- Belmullet Tidal Pool
- Faulmore Bay Beach
- Port Mor Beach

Visit
- Blacksod Lighthouse
- Blacksod Sea Safari
- St Deirbhile's Old Church and Holy Well
- Dún na mBó (Wild Atlantic Way Discovery Point)

Eat
- Talbot's Bar & Restaurant

following the trail, which runs by a fence before turning right; this is all marked.

The next section of trail is a grassy trail with short sections of boardwalk.

At approx. 1.4km the trail turns left and runs adjacent to the cliffs; the cliffs will be to your right-hand side.

Follow the trail and at approx. 2.2km the trail turns left. You will be at your closest point to Illandavuck Island here and will be able to get a glimpse of it from the trail.

The trail from here gradually ascends towards the lookout tower; you will arrive at the tower at approx. 2.9km.

From here the trail is less worn, but the markers are close together. So all you need to do is keep looking ahead for the next one.

Continue to follow the markers and at approx. 3.3km the trail turns left. Before you turn make sure to look out towards the cliffs as you will also see an Éire sign here too.

Following the markers at approx. 3.6km you'll reach the summit marker for Erris Head.

From here continue to follow the markers along a grassy trail, which is often well worn.

At approx. 4.2km, you'll meet your original trail. Turn right here to follow the path back to the car park.

Union Rock

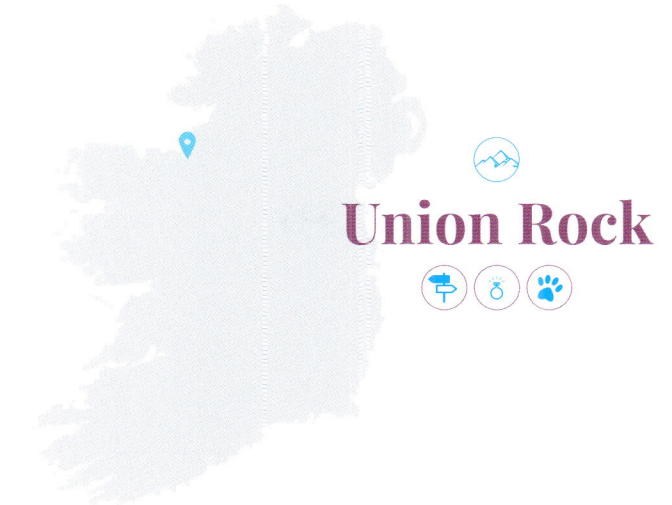

The Union Rock Trail is in Union Wood, a large, forested area, which offers panoramic views of Sligo and beyond from its highest point at Union Rock. This area is steeped in the stories of ancient Ireland. A hike through Union Wood offers views of Knocknarea, the 12m-high stone cairn on the summit which is said to be the tomb of Queen Méabh of Connaught, the Celtic Warrior Queen, best known for her role in the ancient Irish epic, the *Táin Bó Cúailnge* or the 'Cattle Raid of Cooley'. It is said she was buried standing up facing her enemies in Ulster. Also close by are the passage tombs of Carrowmore, dating from the megalithic period, making some of these tombs over 6,000 years old. There are 30 tombs, which means it is the largest complex of megalithic tombs in Ireland.

Union Rock itself is said to have got its name from the local landlord who used to fly a Union Jack flag at the rock when rents were due to be paid. If you look closely, you will find the hole where the flagpole used to be.

What You Need to Know

OSI: 25
Distance: 5.3km
Approx. time: 1.5 hours
Difficulty: easy (well-marked by red arrows or Union Rock signs)
Route type: looped (with a short out-and-back section to the viewpoint of Union Rock)
Starting point: Union Wood, R284 Union, Sligo
Elevation: 130m
Parking: yes, about 30 spaces
Fee: no
Dog friendly: yes, on a leash

Other Hikes in the Area

Benbulbin (p.71)

INCLUDED IN *THE HIKE LIFE* **(BOOK ONE)**
Benbulbin Forest Loop (p.73)

THE TRAIL

From the car park, head towards the barrier, where you will find information signs about the trail.

> **Note:** I recommend taking a photo of the information signs for reference on your hike.

Pass the barrier onto the trail, which is a wide gravel path lined by trees.

At approx. 400m you come to a junction with 3 trails in front of you: follow the trail markers by taking the middle trail.

At approx. 700m you meet a split in the trail, follow the markers left.

This section is a wide stone and grass trail through the forest.

At approx. 2km you will come to another junction where you will follow the markers left.

At approx. 2.2km, at the split in the trail, follow the red arrow up to the left, which will lead you up to the Union Rock boardwalk (this section is the out-and-back part of this trail).

At approx. 2.6km you will meet the boardwalk. This is a truly magically part of this trail, and offers a great photo opportunity along the step section.

At approx. 2.9km you will be at Union Rock. Enjoy the incredible views over to the Ox Mountains, Ballysadare Bay, Knocknarea, Rosses Point, and Benbulbin.

Return back down the boardwalk and along the same trail.

At approx. 3.6km turn left and continue to follow the trail and signs for the car park – you will arrive back to the car park at approx. 5.3km.

PIT STOPS

Swim
- Pol Gorm, Easky

Visit
- Keshcorran Caves (pictured here)
- Carrowkeel Passage Tombs
- Listoghil Cairn (Carrowmore Megalithic Cemetery)
- Strandhill Surf Club
- VOYA Seaweed Baths

Eat
- Tempo Café, Ballysadare
- Pudding Row the Grocer, Easky

In Sligo
- Kate's Kitchen
- Tósta Café
- Milligram Coffee
- Rover Coffee Lab

In Strandhill
- Shells Café
- Fire Dough Pizza (takeaway only)
- Mammy Johnston's (for delicious ice cream!)
- Stoked
- Honestly Farm Kitchen Strandhill

Devil's Chimney Waterfall

Ir. Sruth in Aghaidh An Aird, 'stream against the height'

The Devil's Chimney is a spectacular waterfall located in the Glencar Valley on the Sligo and Leitrim border. The waterfall is 150m tall, making it Ireland's highest. The looped trail is best visited after heavy rainfall, to experience the full majesty of the waterfall, as there will be no flow after a spell of dry weather. The water flow will be visible from the car park so you can check before you set out.

The waterfall's name in Irish, *Sruth in Aghaidh An Aird*, 'stream against the height', comes from the phenomenon that occurs when a southerly wind catches the water and blows it upwards back over the top of the cliff.

This trail takes you through the Glencar Valley, a U-shaped valley, with steep limestone cliffs visible. If you look closely at the cliff face you will see lots of yew trees. These are believed to be among the oldest trees in Ireland.

The best view of the Devil's Chimney is from this trail itself. Sometimes there are two donkeys in a field along this trail, who

What You Need to Know

OSI: 16
Distance: 2.3km
Approx. time: 45 minutes–1 hour
Difficulty: easy
Route type: lollipop circuit (out-and-back with a loop at the end)
Starting point: Devil's Chimney, Tormore Sligo, small layby area along the road
Elevation: 140m
Parking: yes, 3-4 places in a layby
Fee: no
Dog friendly: yes, on a leash

Note: The signs in the area say to keep your dog on a leash until the forest steps. Keep in mind the landscape here is vast with plenty of farmland nearby so this would always be at you and your dog's risk.

PIT STOPS

Swim
- Rosses Point

Visit
- Glencar Waterfall
- Glencar Alpacas
- Gleniff Horseshoe
- The Hot Box Sauna, Rosses Point

Eat
- teaSHED, Glencar
- Vintage Lane Café
- The Driftwood
- The Little Cottage Café

Other Hikes in the Area
Benbulbin (p.71)
Union Rock (p.63)
INCLUDED IN *THE HIKE LIFE* (BOOK ONE)
Benbulbin Forest Walk (p.73)

add an extra bit of character and beauty to the hike.

Note: This trail and additional pit stops make a great day trip in which you'll get to see two beautiful waterfalls. Drive Gleniff Horseshoe, packed with great food, and then take a sunset dip and sauna in Rosses Point – and a day wouldn't get much better than that!

This trail is on private land. Like many landowners, the people here do a great job managing the trail and its upkeep, so please respect their land and leave it as you found it.

THE TRAIL

Note: This trail is marked all along the route with green arrows. There are also clear directions for viewpoints, the waterfall and the car park on the route back.

From the small layby, pass through the small wooden swing gate onto the trail. Follow the narrow gravel trail which runs alongside a house entrance.

After approx. 200m the trail veers left and runs alongside a fence, before gradually rising up through the trees along a forest trail, and a step of steps.

At approx. 800m follow the green arrow right. The trail terrain here is similar: a narrow gravel trail through the forest with another flight of steps.

About 100m after this, the trail turns right.

Pass through a wooden swing gate, following the narrow trail; there is a nice viewpoint along here that's worth enjoying. Continue to follow the trail as it now dips down and rises again.

At approx. 1km, you will see a sign for the waterfall to your right, follow this; this section is short and steep with stone steps.

At approx. 1.2km you will be at the end of this trail, where you can take in the views of the waterfall. The official trail doesn't go directly below the waterfall.

Return back along the trail and at the next junction turn right following the signs for 'views', which will bring you to two more out-and-back vantage points.

You can continue on this loop following the signs for 'car park' to return back down to your original trail.

At approx. 1.6km you will be back on your original trail and can return to your start point.

Benbulbin

Ir. Binn Ghulbain [GÉ], 'beak–shaped peak' or 'Gulban's peak'

What You Need to Know

OSI: 16
Height: 526m
Distance: 11km
Approx. time: 2.5-3 hours
Difficulty: hard
Route type: out-and-back
Starting point: Luke's Bridge
Elevation: 500m
Parking: yes, limited parking (7-8 spaces)
Fee: no
Dog friendly: no

Recommended mountain leader:
Brian Bateson; climbit.ie

Note: There are a number of layby areas here, and there are limited spaces to park at Luke's Bridge. Ensure you do not block gateways or access. I recommend doing this hike off-peak to avoid issues with parking.

Other Hikes in the Area
Devil's Chimney Waterfall (p.67)
Union Rock (p.63)

INCLUDED IN THE HIKE LIFE (BOOK ONE)
Benbulbin Forest Walk (p.73)

Benbulbin, with its flat-topped plateau, is easily one of Ireland's most recognisable mountains. Benbulbin is of course stunning to look up at, but the summit also offers incredible views across nearby and distant landscapes. The first *Hike Life* book included Benbulbin Forest Walk, a great beginner trail that allows you to take in the incredible vista that is Benbulbin. This trail is for those who want to explore the mountain up close and are ready for a challenge.

Benbulbin is steeped in legend and folklore and is the setting for many ancient tales. In the well-known epic, *The Pursuit of Diarmuid and Grainne*, Benbulbin was the fateful lovers' resting place, and the scene of Diarmuid's death, after he was tricked by Fionn Mac Cumhaill into fighting an enchanted boar.

The mountain is also central to Yeats Country, so named as this landscape inspired much of the literature of W. B. Yeats. The poet and Nobel laureate, in the poem 'Under Ben Bulben', expresses his wish to be laid to rest at Drumcliff Churchyard, 'under bare Ben Bulben's head'. You can visit W. B. Yeats' grave at Drumcliff Cemetery near the base of Benbulbin.

Close to Benbulbin is Streedagh Beach, the site of three shipwrecks from the Spanish Armada. The Armada was a fleet of 130 Spanish ships that set sail from Lisbon in 1588, with the purpose of invading England and overthrowing Queen Elizabeth I. Following heavy losses in fierce sea battles in the English

Channel, the remaining ships in the Armada returned via the west coast of Ireland. Bad weather conditions led to the wreckage of as many as 28 ships along the west coast. One of the ships wrecked at Streedagh Beach, the *San Pedro*, was captained by Francisco de Cueller who gave an incredible account of his experiences in the fleet, his subsequent survival in Ireland and eventual return to Spain.

THE TRAIL

Note: This trail is not marked. I recommend using navigation tools. Even on a nice clear day having these tools is important.

Being aware of the weather forecast is essential for this hike. Due to Benbulbin's positioning and shape it can be very dangerous and it's easy to get disorientated here in poor visibilty. Avoid this route in unsuitable weather and of course be prepared to turn back in adverse conditions. The mountain isn't going anywhere!

Starting from Luke's Bridge, pass over the bridge and continue up along the road as it gets steep; the river will be on your right-hand side.

At approx. 80m keep right as the road splits.

After approx. 800m turn right, passing over a bridge, and almost immediately (10m) at the junction turn right, following this rocky path.

At approx. 1km, with Benbulbin towering in front of you, turn left.

The path here is easy to follow: it is a

PIT STOPS

Swim
- Bishop's Pool
- Rosses Point

Visit
- Glenariff Horseshoe
- Mullaghmore Beach (for surfing)
- Glencar Waterfall
- Eagle's Rock
- Classiebawn Castle Viewpoint
- Island View Riding Stables
- Streedagh Beach
- The Hot Box Sauna, Rosses Point

Eat
- The Jam Pot Café, Grange
- Vintage Lane Café
- The Driftwood
- The Little Cottage Café

hard-surfaced and stony trail.

At approx. 1.6km the hard-surfaced terrain ends, and this next section is extremely boggy through the grass.

Follow the vaguely worn trail working its way towards the stream/gully head. The trail dips in and out of visibility here.

At approx. 1.9km you will begin your ascent: there is a vague zigzag trail which runs up alongside the stream, which will be to your left-hand side.

At approx. 2.7km you will be at the top of the stream where the trail then veers right and climbs up onto the long summit plateau.

At approx. 2.8km, the trail becomes relatively level with only a slight ascent and descent, as you hike across the mountain plateau to the summit marker.

the route is boggy and grassy with exposed drops to your right-hand side.

Note: This section feels long. However, you will be sustained by the amazing views over to the Benwiskin and Slievemore summits.

At approx. 4.4km, follow the trail as it veers left towards the summit marker.

At approx. 4.8km you will reach the summit marker.

Note: An out-and-back from here is also a popular route.

From the summit marker continue along the boggy and vague trail towards Benbulbin Head; there is little to no change in gradient along this section.

You should reach Benbulbin Head at approx. 5.8km.

Note: Be mindful of the severe drops at this section.

Return the way you came.

Note: There are amazing viewpoints all along this trail but be extremely cautious when exploring and keep a safe distance from the edge. You will get lovely pictures without needing to go too close! Be safe and smart.

Mullaghgarve Mass Rock
at Sliabh An Iarainn
Ir. Sliabh An Iarainn, 'mountain of the iron'

Sliabh an Iarainn takes its name from the abundant mineral resources in the area, including coal, which was mined at Arigna and iron ore, mined at the base of the mountain from the 1600s for nearly 300 years. According to local legend the iron mines were worked by Goibniu, the metal-smithing god of the Tuatha Dé Danann, a supernatural race of pre-Christian Ireland. In fact, the mountain has a long association with the Tuatha Dé Danann. The *Book of Invasions* describes the Tuatha Dé Danann arriving in Ireland by air in floating ships, which they landed on the summit of Sliabh an Iarainn. In more recent history the iron ore from the mountain is thought to have made the famous Ha'penny Bridge on the River Liffey in Dublin.

Mass rocks are a common feature on the mountains of Ireland. Mass rocks are stone altars, used to celebrate Catholic Mass in secret, in response to the penal laws of the seventeenth and 18th century. Some of the mass rocks were taken from churches and placed in remote locations, others were used as they were. There are many records of massacres at mass rock locations, as worshippers were caught by Crown soldiers, in the crime of celebrating

What You Need to Know
OSI: 26
Distance: 3.2km
Approx. time: 1 hour
Difficulty: easy-moderate (due to the steep sections at the mass rock)
Route type: lollipop circuit (out-and-back with a small loop section at the mass rock)
Starting point: Sliabh An Iarainn and Mullaghgarve Mass Rock Walks, Leitrim
Elevation: 200m
Parking: yes, 15 spaces (height barrier 2m)
Fee: no
Dog friendly: no

Other Hikes in the Area

Union Rock (p.63)

INCLUDED IN *THE HIKE LIFE* (BOOK ONE)
Cuilcagh (p.213)

MORE TO EXPLORE
Sliabh an Iarainn

Mass. Still, some mass rocks are used to this day on special feast days.

Make sure you bring food with you on your hike, as according to local legend there is an intense hunger that can afflict you on Sliabh an Iarainn, especially if you walk on a legendary 'fear-gorta stone' (hungry-man stone) at the base of Sliabh an Iarainn.

THE TRAIL

Note: The entire route is marked by black metre posts with a mass rock symbol.

From the car park turn right following the sign for 'mass rock'.

You will come to a gate with signage and an information board about the hike. Take a picture of this for reference during your hike.

Pass through the metal swing gate to the left-hand side of the large farm gate.

Follow the wide gravel trail. At about 360m you will come to another gate, pass over the stile that's to the right of this gate.

At approx. 470m, you will come to another gate; you'll need to pass over the stile to the right of it.

Continue to follow the wide gravel trail which is marked.

At approx. 1km the trail turns left and becomes a narrow gravel path.

At approx. 1.2km the trail turns into a narrow, boggy and grassy trail with a short section of boardwalk.

At approx. 1.5km, you will reach the mass rock, which I like to loop anti-clockwise. Follow the trail up to the right: it is a short but very steep climb.

Note: After rainfall it can be slippery, and scrambling on hands may be required in sections here.

At approx. 1.6km you will be at the small stone altar.

Continue down from here along the steep stones which act as steps, being mindful to watch your step, and at the bottom of the steps immediately turn left to loop the rock.

Return along the route you came

PIT STOPS

Visit
- Arigna Mining Experience
- The Shed Distillery of PJ Rigney
- Drumherny Woodland Hideaway
- Acres Lake Floating Boardwalk
- Sweathouse Battlebridge
- Lough Key Forest & Activity Park

Eat
- Jinny's Bakery & Tearoom at Acres
- Èabha's Street Kitchen
- The Jackaloupe Café

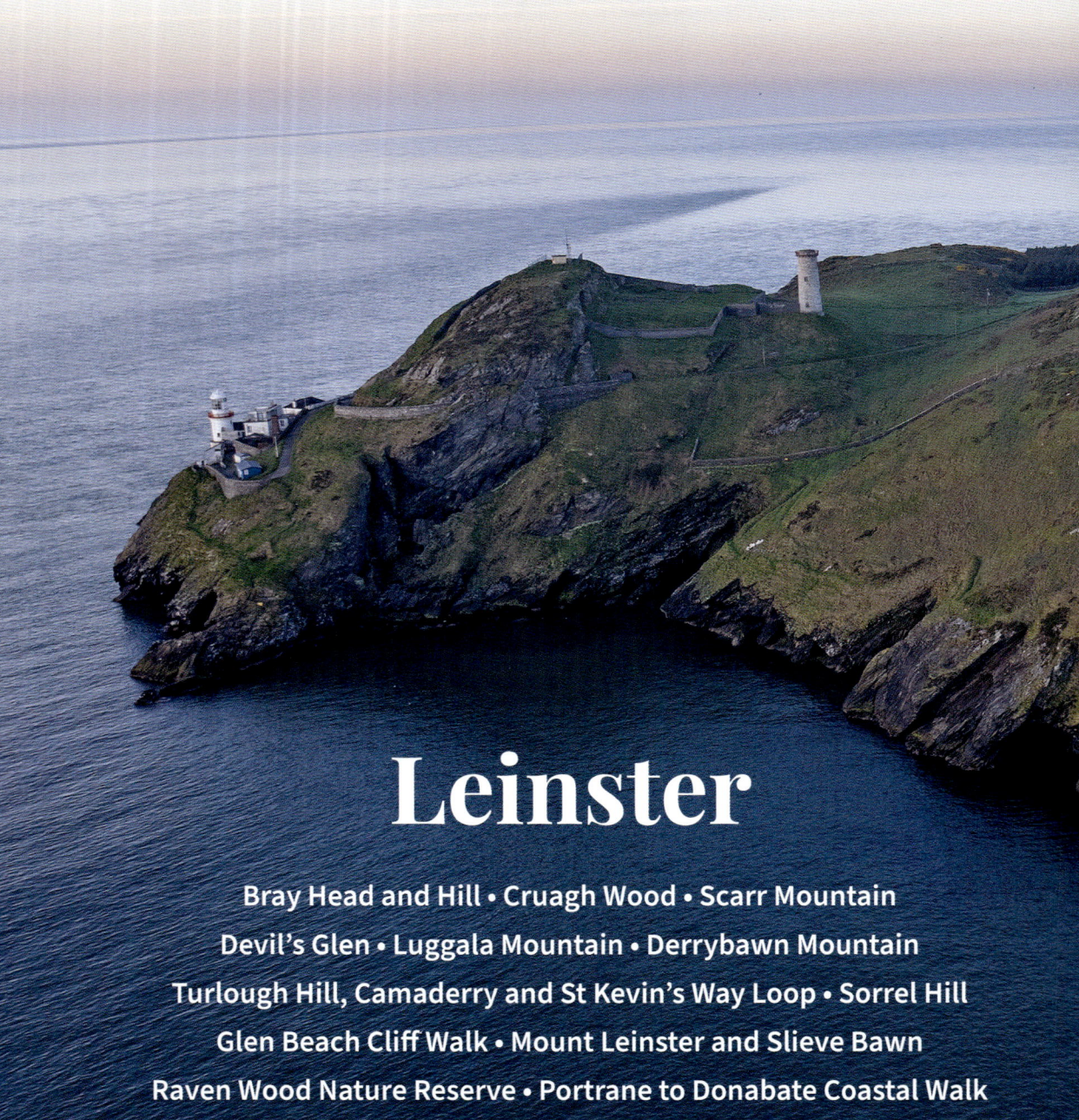

Leinster

Bray Head and Hill • Cruagh Wood • Scarr Mountain
Devil's Glen • Luggala Mountain • Derrybawn Mountain
Turlough Hill, Camaderry and St Kevin's Way Loop • Sorrel Hill
Glen Beach Cliff Walk • Mount Leinster and Slieve Bawn
Raven Wood Nature Reserve • Portrane to Donabate Coastal Walk
Mullaghmeen

Bray Head and Hill

Ir. Ceann Bhré

Bray Head is a headland where the Wicklow Mountains meet the sea. The Bray to Greystones coastal walk has been closed for a number of years due to rock fall but this trail alternative is just as good with heaps of history and even better scenery.

The trail offers wonderful views of the Irish Sea, Dublin Bay and the Wicklow Mountains. On the trail you will pass what is left of the Bray chairlift. The chairlift was opened in 1952 by the businessman Eamonn Quinn to bring patrons to the Eagle's Nest Restaurant and Ballroom, located halfway up Bray Head. It operated until the 1970s. At the summit there is a large cross, erected in 1950. It is a site of pilgrimage on Good Friday each year.

The turnaround point for the trail today is Bray Head Hill (240m), not to be confused with Bray Head Cross (197m). This is a peak that is often overlooked along this trail and is easy to miss; it is marked by a summit marker and offers great views down to Greystones. There

What You Need to Know

OSI: 56
Height: 240m (Bray Hill)
Distance: 5.6km (8.8km from the dart)
Approx. time: 1.5 hours
Difficulty: moderate, however the ascents and descerts from Bray Head are strenuous
Route type: out-and-back
Starting point: Cliff Walk car park, Raheen Park, Newcourt, Bray
Elevation: 260m
Parking: yes, about 80 spaces
Fee: no
Dog friendly: yes, on a leash

Other Hikes in the Area

INCLUDED IN *THE HIKE LIFE* **(BOOK ONE)**
Great and Little Sugarloaf (p.111)

used to be a 15-foot obelisk monument on this hill in honour of Queen Victoria's Diamond Jubilee in 1897. However, in 1933 unknown men blew it up.

> **Public Transport:** There are multiple buses to Bray and of course the dart. Starting from the dart station the hike would be 8.8km.

Starting from Bray Seafront:
You can start from the end of the seafront under Bray Head where the 'Bray Head Cliff Walk' pin begins. Note that along here it is on-street parking and fees may apply depending on the day and time.

Follow the road which passes by private houses to the right and then a barrier onto a paved trail.

The trail gradually inclines and goes over a bridge. To your right you'll see the cliff walk car park which is free, where I begin the trail description.

THE TRAIL

Leaving from Cliff Walk car park through the gap in the stone wall, turn right and you'll see a raised paved trail that leads to steps and an opening in the wall on the right.

This distinctive trail starts with a section of paved steps before turning rocky with exposed tree roots as you go up through the forest. This section can be slippery after rainfall.

PIT STOPS in Bray

Swim
- Bray Beach
- Naylor's Cove

Visit
- Killruddery House & Gardens
- Helios Sauna

Eat
- Catalyst Coffee – Beach
- Daata Bray
- The Harbour Bar
- Copper + Straw
- Nine, Bray

PIT STOPS in Greystones

Swim
- The Cove

Visit
- Fad Saoil Saunas
- The Barrel Sauna

Eat
- The Fat Fox
- Scéal Bakery
- The Happy Pear
- The Boatyard Market food trucks – The Yellov, Burrito Box and No. 84 Woodfire

At approx. 350m the trail splits, straight ahead (slightly steeper) or to the right. Both trails rejoin, so take which one suits you.

You'll arrive at an opening in the forest, a perfect spot to take a break in the shade or shelter depending on the day.

Continue upwards along the path. The cross will soon come into view as you leave the forest shelter. The trail becomes very narrow and rocky running up between the gorse.

At approx. 650m you'll come to a group of trees just below the summit; here the trail veers slightly right and winds up to the summit cross.

At approx. 800m you will be at the summit cross. Take time to enjoy the summit. Once you're ready to continue, follow the upper Cliff Walk trail; the sea will be to your left-hand side.

After only approx. 100m you'll come to a gate with signage for the Bray Head Loop Trail; here you need to pass through the small metal gate to the right-hand side.

Follow this wide stony trail, which is marked by red arrows.

At approx. 2.4km the trail meets a fence and begins to run alongside it. Approx. 100m after this, you'll see red arrows and a trail going right. However, this is where we leave the red markers and continue straight along the fence; you will see that there is a worn grassy trail along here.

Following the fence line you'll arrive at a small metal gate; pass through this, ensuring you close it afterwards.

The narrow rocky trail through the ferns and shrubbery will lead you up to Bray Hill and the summit marker. Make sure to take in the views of Greystones and the north beach; this is marked on Google as Trigonometric Point Ballynamaddagh.

Return the way you came.

Cruagh Wood
Ir. Coill Na Craobhai

Cruagh Woods, located in the Dublin Mountains, offer wonderful views of Dublin City, Dun Laoghaire and Howth. Official records of Cruagh Woods date back to 1184, when Prince John, son of King Henry II, granted the Cruagh to the See of Dublin. Today the area is managed by Coillte on behalf of the state.

Nearby is Tibradden hill, another great hike that you can add onto this one or do on another day. The summit is marked by a prehistoric chambered cairn, believed to be from the Bronze Age or even as far back as the neolithic period.

They are a favourite of mine near Dublin City, and I love exploring these forests. It is ideal if you want to get out on a rainy day with the dogs. It is a very popular spot so try to go on off-peak days, or early on weekends to secure a parking spot.

What You Need to Know
OSI: 50
Height: 521m (Cruagh Mountain)
Distance: 5.5km
Approx. time: 1-1.5 hours
Difficulty: easy
Route type: looped
Starting point: Cruagh Nature Walk
Elevation: 180m
Parking: yes, approx. 35 spaces
Fee: no
Dog friendly: yes, on a leash

Other Hikes in the Area
INCLUDED IN *THE HIKE LIFE* (BOOK ONE)
Fairy Castle Loop, Ticknock (p.95)
Lough Bray (p.91)
MORE TO EXPLORE
Tibradden (multiple trail options)
Montpelier Loop (4.2km)

THE TRAIL

> **Note:** This is a marked Slí na Sláinte trail, turning to white markers for some of the summit trail.

From the car park, pass by the barrier onto the forest road, which is a wide hard surface gravel road.

At approx. 180m, keep straight and follow the forest road.

At approx. 1km at the junction, take the trail to the right following the markers.

At approx. 2km leave the Slí na Sláinte markers and turn left along a narrow trail; there are stone steps that lead up onto a boardwalk.

Along this section there is 700m of beautiful boardwalk.

The boardwalk ends and it meets a wide gravel rocky trail. At this junction turn right and then almost immediately there is a trail to your left.

> **Note:** From here this section of trail is a short 600m out-and-back to the summit cairn, returning back to this exact point - which is called The Point - to continue on.

To reach the summit, follow this trail to your left; it is a very distinctive narrow and rocky trail.

At approx. 2.9km at the corner of the fence (to your left-hand side), you will come to a junction with three trails in front of you. Here you need to take the middle trail.

PIT STOPS

Swim
- Vico Bathing Place
- Forty Foot
- Seapoint Beach
- Lough Bray Upper and Lower

Visit
- Glencullen Adventure Park (The GAP) - mountain biking trails
- Zipit Forest Adventures

Eat
- Daily Grind Coffee
- Timbertrove Café
- The Hazel House
- Woodruff
- Fire & Stone

Follow this until you reach the summit cairn at approx. 3km.

Return back all the way down the narrow trail to The Point then turn left and continue along this wide and rocky gravel path.

This section of trail is stunning. With a forest to your right-hand side, it descends gradually back down into the forest.

At approx. 4.5km, turn right down through a wide trail through the forest and after approx. 200m at the next junction, turn left onto a forest road following the Slí na Sláinte signs.

At approx. 5.3km you turn left back down towards the car park.

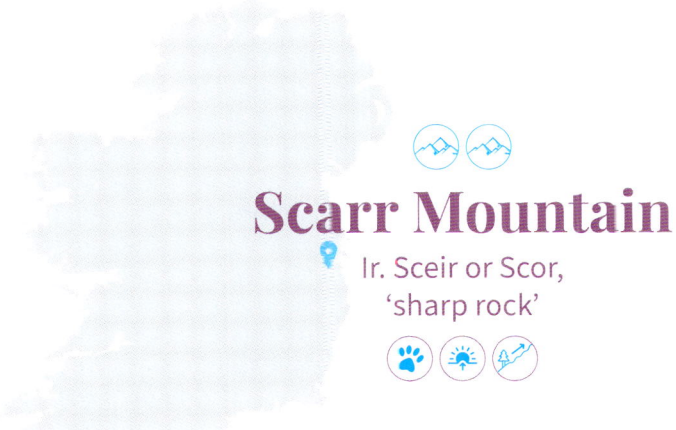

Scarr Mountain

Ir. Sceir or Scor, 'sharp rock'

Scarr Mountain is a peak that often gets overlooked in the Wicklow Mountains. The beauty of Scarr is it's a hike with several routes up, so depending on what kind of adventure you want there are plenty of options: it offers great panoramic views and it's easily accessible from the east side of the Wicklow Mountains coming from Dublin City.

Scarr Mountain offers wonderful views of Glenmacnass Valley, which is where I would recommend starting. This is a glaciated U-shaped valley with steep cliff sides. The valley is home to the impressive 80m-high Glenmacnass Waterfall and Scarr summit also offers views over towards Lough Dan, a glacial ribbon lake, and of course clear views out towards the Irish Sea, the Sugarloaf and Bray hills. In short, on one side you have the rolling hills and peaks of the Wicklow Mountains and on the other side you're looking out to the sea, which is why I love this one at sunrise in particular.

The route I'm showcasing is the most

What You Need to Know

OSI: 56
Height: 641m
Distance: 5.5km
Approx. time: 1.5–2 hours
Difficulty: moderate
Route type: out-and-back
Starting point: Glenmacnass Waterfall car park
Elevation: 270m
Parking: yes, about 25-30 spaces
Fee: no
Dog friendly: yes, on a leash

Other Hikes in the Area

Turlough Hill, Camaderry and St Kevin's Way Loop (p.111)

INCLUDED IN *THE HIKE LIFE* (BOOK ONE)
Tonelagee (p.117)

MORE TO EXPLORE
Scarr Mountain via Paddock Hill (Laragh Village) (11.5km)
Vartry Trails (Woodland 3.3km, Upper 6.4km, Lower 7.2km)

PIT STOPS
Visit
- Glenmacnass Waterfall
- Glendalough Monastic Site and Visitor Centre
- Lough Tay Viewpoint
- Victor's Way
- K2Alpacas

Eat
- The Roundwood Stores
- Turquoise Café & Eatery
- The Wicklow Heather Restaurant
- Lynhams of Laragh
- The Coach House
- Glendalough Green Café

direct out-and-back one. It is very boggy almost all year round so appropriate footwear is essential. There are also a lot of deer in this area. Every time I've hiked here, no matter what time of day, I've seen hundreds. Please be mindful of their space and ensure you do keep your dog on a leash at all times.

THE TRAIL

The trail is worn, but the large open boggy sections can make it hard to follow. The higher you go, the more distinct the trail becomes. A form of navigation is advised.

Starting from the car park, carefully cross the road where you will see a narrow trail that dips off the road and quickly begins to ascend.

The route runs up steeply here on a narrow boggy trail cut into the mountain slope.

At approx. 1.3km keep right (the left trail is for Kanturk Summit), following the route as it keeps ascending and passing over Scarr North-West Top.

When you reach approx. 1.8km there are some great views down onto Glenmacnass Waterfall.

At approx. 2.6km the trail splits. Here you need to keep right for the final ascent to Scarr Summit.

> **Note:** The trail split here catches a lot of people out on the way down, so remember that at approx. 100m down from the summit the trails splits and you need to keep left to return the way you came.

You will reach Scarr Summit where there is a small cairn at approx. 2.75km.

Return the way you came.

Devil's Glen

The Devil's Glen is a big forest dissected by a large gorge formed by the River Vartry. According to local legend, the area of Devil's Glen was once fertile, rolling countryside, ruled by a powerful Chieftain. The Chieftain had a beautiful daughter called Flora, who despite many suitors refused all offers of marriage. One day a handsome stranger arrived, laden with gold and jewels, but Flora again refused his offer of marriage. The suitor flew into a rage, revealing himself to be the Devil. In retribution, he tore up the land, scattered it with rocks and thus created the rugged landscape evident today. Hence its name: Devil's Glen. Geologists, of course, would tell us that the valley was formed by retreating ice at the end of the Ice Age.

Along a section of this trail are quotes by renowned Irish poet and Nobel laureate Seamus Heaney, who lived in the gate lodge of the nearby Glanmore Castle in the 1970s and later bought a holiday home in the area. You can stop and read quotes from some of Heaney's

What You Need to Know

OSI: 56
Distance: 5.7km
Approx. time: 1.5-2 hours
Difficulty: easy
Route type: looped
Starting point: Devil's Glen car park, which is past the entrance car park
Elevation: 210m
Parking: yes
Fee: no
Dog friendly: yes, on a leash

Other Hikes in the Area

Glen Beach Cliff Walk (p.121)
Derrybawn Mountain (p.105)
Turlough Hill, Camaderry and St Kevins Way Loop (p.111)

INCLUDED IN *THE HIKE LIFE* (BOOK ONE)
Djouce via Ballinastoe Woods (p.105)
Glendalough Spinc and Glenealo Valley Loop (p.121)

writings as you follow this trail. It is said that some of Heaney's finest poems were inspired by his time here. He spoke about the 'strange loneliness' of the Devil's Glen, which gives you something to contemplate on your hike.

The final plaque at the waterfall viewpoint reads 'when we find the ring, I'll propose', which is why I think this spot is the engagement spot of all spots in Ireland!

THE TRAIL

> **Note:** This trail is great after rain to make the waterfall even more impressive. But it can also get mucky and waterlogged in some places. The trail also runs beside the river for a large part of this hike and the water is fast moving.

I like doing the hike clockwise so you're walking towards the waterfall along the upper track where you get lovely views before returning alongside the river on the lower path.

From the Devil's Glen car park (past the first car park) you can start from a few different directions to get onto the trail, but I suggest taking the route which starts at the back of the car park where there is a red arrow and a narrow trail which leads you straight onto the hike.

Along this trail, follow the red arrows, until approx. 300m when you'll see a red arrow directing you down to the right: pass this and keep going straight, about 50m after this keep right at the junction.

From here follow the trail which is a mix of mud paths, footbridges and a beautiful rock arch. Through the trees you will also get views of the valley to your right. This section is marked by red arrows. At approx. 1.8km there is a junction where you will need to keep right and follow the 'waterfall' sign.

This trail gradually descends bringing you down to the river. At approx. 2.1km the trail meets the river at a Y junction. Keep

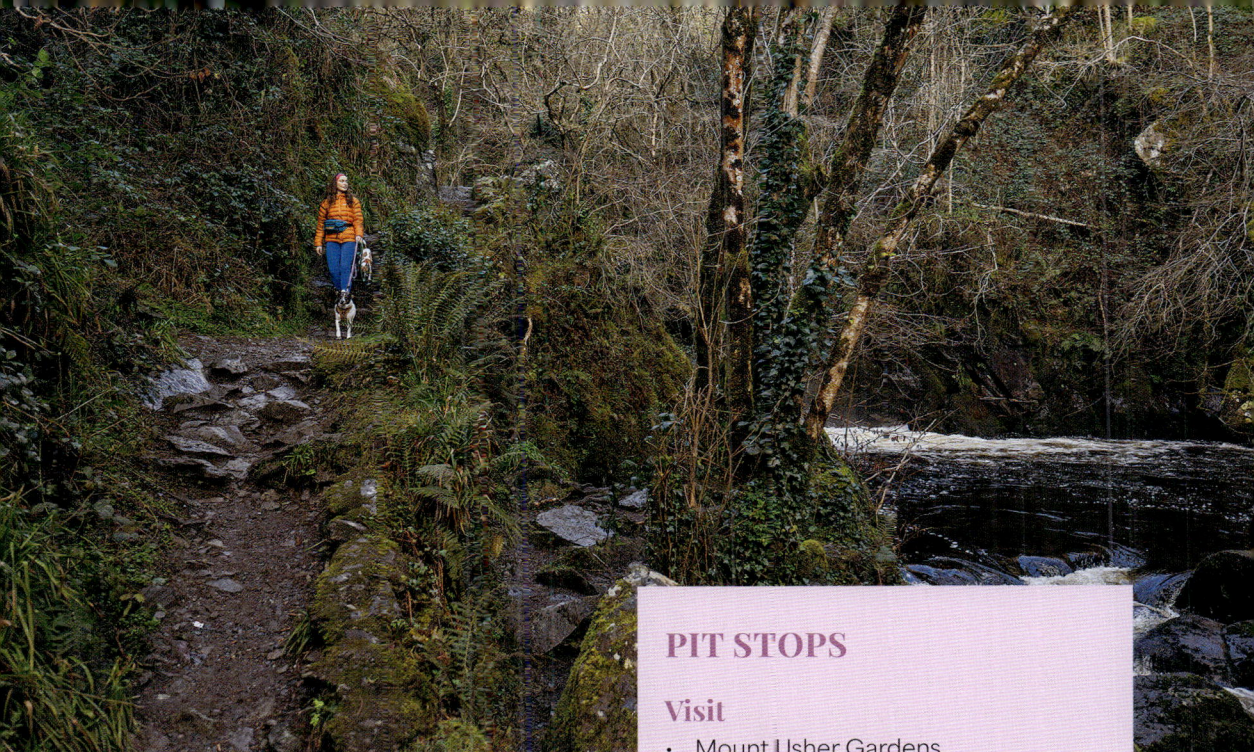

straight to walk alongside the river, which will be to your right-hand side.

This section of trail is narrow and mucky with some exposed tree roots.

At approx. 2.3km you'll reach a set of stone steps leading up to the waterfall viewpoint where you can take in the marvellous views of the Devil's Glen Waterfall.

From this point, return along the trail and at approx. 300m at the Y junction keep left. You're now returning to the car park alongside the river (to your left).

In approx. 4.5km you'll see another plaque and steps up to your right: don't take this, continue on straight.

Along the trail at approx. 4.7km there's a lovely bench on the riverbank, a perfect spot on the way back to relax.

Keep following the trail and at approx. 5.2km, at the junction, turn right for the uphill gradual push back to the car park. Pass by the barrier, and you'll see the car park on your right.

PIT STOPS

Visit
- Mount Usher Gardens
- Beyond the Trees Avondale
- K2Alpacas

Eat
- Joly's Garden Centre and Café
- Red Eye Coffee
- The Roundwood Stores
- The WoodPecker Bar & Restaurant

See Glen Beach Cliff Walk (p.121) for more nearby suggestions.

Leinster | 99

Luggala Mountain

Ir. Log an Lá,
'Hollow of the hill' (pronounced 'Lug-a-law')

Luggala mountain is part of the Luggala estate, a 5,000-acre estate that was home to the Guinness family. The estate was also the location for many films and television series including *Braveheart* and *Vikings*. The trail offers wonderful views of Lough Tay and the Sally Gap. Lough Tay is also known as 'Guinness Lake', with its dark waters and white sand beach resembling a pint of Guinness. This is especially the case when viewed from Luggala. The Sally Gap is an east-west pass on the Wicklow Mountains; the road was built by the British army after the 1798 Rebellion as a way to flush out rebels hiding in the hills of Wicklow and to this day it is known as the Military Road.

Luggala is on private land like a lot of Irish peaks and trails. There is an option to go via Luggala estate for a longer hike, but take note that access to this trail is open only at certain times. The route I take is the most direct one; it's on the west side of the mountain from the R115.

Check the Luggala estate for updates on access and rules (luggala.com).

What You Need to Know

OSI: 56
Height: 595m
Distance: 4.4km
Approx. time: 1.5–2 hours
Difficulty: moderate
Route type: out-and-back
Starting point: parking area, Old Military Road, Cloghoge, Co. Wicklow
Elevation: 135m
Parking: yes, 10 spaces
Fee: no
Dog friendly: no

Other Hikes in the Area

Scarr Mountain (p.93)

INCLUDED IN *THE HIKE LIFE* (BOOK ONE)
Djouce via Ballinastoe Woods (p.105)
Lough Bray Loop (p.91)

Leinster | 101 |

THE TRAIL

Some form of navigation is necessary as the trail is unmarked with exposed cliffs at the summit area. The route to the summit is boggy and the trail dips in and out of being visible.

Carefully cross the road where you will see a trail begin and a small sign about the Luggala Estate.

The trail from here meanders up, very gradually ascending towards the summit.

At approx. 2.2km you'll reach Luggala summit, where you will be greeted by incredible views over Lough Tay.

There are some really nice vantage points here; take time to sit and enjoy the views across to Djouce, War Hill and Ballinastoe Woodland.

Return the way you came.

PIT STOPS

Swim
- Lough Bray Upper

Visit
- Lough Tay Viewpoint
- *P.S. I Love You* Bridge (for fans of the movie)
- Glenmacnass Waterfall
- Victor's Way
- Ballinastoe Woods sleeper steps

Eat
- The Roundwood Stores
- Turquoise Café & Eatery
- Trails Café

Derrybawn Mountain

Ir. Doire Bána,
'oak-grove of Badbgna'

This trail is a photographer's dream, with stunning views of the surrounding Wicklow mountains and lakes. It offers a great way to explore Glendalough while avoiding the tourists and the busy car parks of the upper lake. It loops down by the Poulanass Waterfall, Glendalough Lake and the Round Tower, which are iconic spots and the only busy sections along this hike. Glendalough is home to one of Ireland's most important monastic sites, a 'monastic city' established by St Kevin in the 6th century. Central to this heritage site, is the 30m-high Round Tower, thought to be over a thousand years old. The oak forests on the lower slopes of Derrybawn Mountain are part of the Glendalough Wood Nature Reserve, established in 1988, and the Wicklow Mountains National Park.

There is an option to make this hike longer, extending along Derrybawn Ridge to Mullacor, looping onto the Spinc trail. This is a great option for those looking for a more challenging and longer hike, and

What You Need to Know

OSI: 56
Height: 476
Distance: 10.4km
Approx. time: 5-6 hours
Difficulty: moderate-hard
Route type: looped
Starting point: Laragh free car park, Brockagh, Wicklow
Elevation: 400m
Parking: yes; the car park has a height restriction barrier, it is open 8am-8pm every day
Fee: no
Dog friendly: yes, on a leash

Other Hikes in the Area

Scarr Mountain (p.93)
Turlough Hill, Camaderry and St Kevins Way Loop (p.111)

INCLUDED IN *THE HIKE LIFE* (BOOK ONE)
Tonelagee and Lough Ouler (p.117)
Glendalough Spinc and Glenealo Valley Loop (p.121)

Leinster [105]

it is one I would definitely recommend if you have time.

There is also an option to make this hike shorter and easier, by doing the lower Derrybawn Woodland Loop (8km). This route starts from the same car park, but omits the summit, following the orange arrows. It is truly stunning and one of my favourite routes for Hike Life meet-ups, especially dog-friendly ones.

This is a very quiet trail, and many times along the forest section I have seen deer, pine martens and foxes so be sure to keep an eye out and keep your dogs on a leash.

THE TRAIL

From the car park turn left over Derrybawn Bridge, following the road as it ends at Glendalough Woollen Mills. Pass by on the left-hand side.

Follow the wide gravel path as it winds up through the trees.

At approx. 670m keep left, passing by the wooden barrier. Continue following the wide gravel path as it rises and winds its way up through the forest.

At approx. 1km pass through a metal gate.

PIT STOPS

Swim
- Coolalingo Waterfalls

Visit
- Bosca Beatha, mobile sauna
- Glendalough Monastic Site and Visitor Centre (this is along the trail)
- Glendalough Upper Lake
- Powerscourt Waterfall
- St Kevin's Lead and Zinc Mine
- Beyond the Trees Avondale

Eat
- The Glenmalure Lodge
- The Roundwood Stores
- The Coach House Gastro Pub
- The Wicklow Heather
- Glendalough Green Café
- Hollywood Café

Continue to follow the wide gravel path, as it zigzags up the hillside

At approx. 1.9km pass through another metal gate.

From here, continue following the orange waymarker.

At approx. 2.2km, at this junction turn left, leaving the orange waymarkers.

Note: To do the shorter loop, keep following the orange waymarkers.

Continuing on, follow this gravel track up through the trees.

At approx. 2.6km make a sharp turn right along a forest trail. Then, at approx 3.4km there will be a wide trail to your left; follow this steep shortcut up to the upper trail.

At the top, turn right to follow the stony and grassy path.

At approx. 4.1km you will see a narrow trail to your left, which leads up to Derrybawn summit.

Note: This trail is steep, mucky and rocky. There is a false peak 200m from the summit.

At approx. 4.6km you will reach the cairn at the summit of Derrybawn.

Enjoy the views, return back down the trail you came up.

At approx. 150m down from the summit you will see a trail to the left: this rocky and narrow trail leads down the hillside towards the Spinc.

Note: It's a very steep descent over rocky and boggy terrain, concentration is required. Along the trail, there is also an old fence with barbed wire, be so careful.

At approx. 5.4km, you will come down onto a forest road. There is the option here to turn right and follow the road down or cross the road and take the narrow shortcut down through the trees. This shortcut is about 150m: it's a steep descent on rocky terrain through the trees and ferns.

You will come out onto a forest road, then turn left. From here you can follow the orange waymarkers again.

Continue to follow the road across the bridge, turning right after the bridge and passing the wooden barrier.

Follow this gravel trail down along the river. You will come to steps leading down by Poulanass Waterfall to your right.

At approx. 6.4km you will arrive at Glendalough Upper Lake car park and lake area.

Note: A short 100m detour from this loop is Glendalough Lake, a great spot to take a break; there are also toilets and other amenities at the car park at the Upper Lake.

Otherwise, to keep on the route, turn right, following the orange waymarkers.

This next section is a hard-surfaced path leading the entire way back onto your original trail and the car park.

Note: This section does feel long, but you pass by Glendalough Round Tower, Cathedral, Visitor Centre and St Saviour's Priory. It is worth stopping to enjoy this important historical site and break up this section of the route.

Turlough Hill, Camaderry and St Kevin's Way Loop

Ir: Sliabh Céim an Doire, 'step/pass of the oak-wood'

Camaderry is located in the southern part of the Wicklow Mountains. Camaderry's neighbouring summit, Turlough Hill, is home to Ireland's only pumped-storage hydroelectric plant. Water is pumped from a lower to a higher elevation reservoir using renewable energy sources, to be released during periods of high electricity demand: the power station can generate 292 megawatts of electricity at such times of peak demand. Lough Nahanagan, which lies between Camaderry and Turlough, is a small corrie lake, with an interesting name, which has been translated to mean 'lake of the otters' or 'lake of the water monster'. Thus, it might be that the lake is associated with the dobhar-chú from Irish mythology, a half-man, half-water creature (often depicted as an otter), which moved between the human and fairy worlds. The dobhar-chú are said to emit a loud whistling or screeching sound, using this noise to lure people to the water and their death!

For an amazing 3-in-1 hike, you can take in Turlough Hill across to Camaderry and then walk along the St Kevin's Way as you loop back.

What You Need to Know

OSI: 56
Height: 699m
Distance: 15.7km
Approx. time: 4 hours
Difficulty: moderate-hard (due to distance)
Route type: looped
Starting point: Wicklow Mountains Viewing Platform car park
Elevation: 615m
Parking: yes, two large car parks
Fee: no
Dog friendly: yes, on a leash (but this trail is very long)

Recommended mountain leader:
Cindy; adventure.ie
Simon; adventureburn.com
Kathryn; tworockoutdoor.ie

You can do each of these individually (details below), pair them up or do all three as described; as a 3-in-1 it really is one of my favourite loops.

The views walking along the top of Camaderry down towards Glendalough are sensational: Camaderry is positioned so perfectly within the Wicklow Mountains that with this hike you're able to enjoy this incredible panoramic view with layers of mountains to your right and left. I always think how it's the perfect spot to play a game of Name That Mountain – because the view allows you to almost see them all.

Then you have St Kevin's Way, which is one of my favourite long-distance trails; it's full of great history and fantastic dipping spots. It was also one of the hikes I did for the TV series Tracks and Trails.

PIT STOPS

Swim
- Glendasan – the river has some nice rock pools (lovely for dipping the feet)
- St Kevin's Pool

Visit
- Glendalough Monastic Site and Visitor Centre
- Glendalough Upper Lake

Eat
- The Roundwood Stores
- The Wicklow Heather
- Glendalough Green Café
- Hollywood Café (if returning towards N81)

THE TRAIL

Note: You will need navigational tools for this hike; here serves only as a general overview of the loop.

From the car park walk up the boardwalk marked by a Wicklow Mountains National Park sign, leading to the upper car park.

From here, veer right, cutting across the car park and onto the tarmac road. There is a blue gate to your left.

Pass to the right of the gate. Now follow this tarmac road up, keeping right at the split.

At approx. 3.2km, the tarmac road ends. Your navigational tools will be essential from here. Turn left up to a large fence surrounding Turlough Hill reservoir. Walk up to the fence and the trail turns right; the terrain from here turns into a rocky and boggy narrow trail, which goes along the perimeter of the reservoir. The fence will be to your left-hand side.

At approx. 3.9km, the trail leaves the fence and now continues across towards Camaderry summit.

This section is vaguely worn; it's narrow, grassy and very boggy and there is a section of eroded bog too, and this is where the trail can become hard to see.

At approx. 5.2km the route reaches Camaderry summit, which is marked by a large rock.

The trail now continues on towards Camaderry SE top (677m) along a rocky and exposed stone trail.

Other Hikes in the Area

INCLUDED IN *THE HIKE LIFE* (BOOK ONE)
Tonelagee and Lough Ouler (p 17) (these start from the same car park)

MORE TO EXPLORE
Turlough Hill out-and-back (6.4km)
St Kevin's Way (26km) (can be broken into sections)

At approx. 6.4km, the height of Camaderry SE top is marked by a large rock pile.

From here the trail continues down along a spur towards Glendalough monastic village.

You will be descending along a narrow boggy trail; there are some rocks where you might find you need to use your hands to get over.

The trail then levels out for a time along a grassy track before descending again and weaving down through a forest.

At approx. 9.8km you'll see a sign for the Miner's Way; you need to turn left and follow this.

This section is a narrow forest trail with some exposed tree roots and a stretch of boardwalk. Take care, as the boardwalk can be slippery.

At approx. 10.2km the trail comes out onto a minor road; turn left here. Now you're on St Kevin's Way and the Miner's Way; at this stage it is a minor road going up the Glendasan valley, with the river to your right-hand side.

After passing St Kevin's lead and zinc mine, the trail terrain changes into a narrow track of stone steps, a boardwalk and loose rock running uphill with the river on its right-hand side.

At approx. 11.6km there is a slip trail right which you can take to see the river (this is an out-and-back section).

At approx. 12.2km, you will stop following the Miner's Way (as it turns right), but still continue to follow trail signs for St Kevin's Way; you will pass by the lead and zinc mines, cross over St Kevin's bridge, pass a large forest to your right-hand side and Turlough Hill power station and Lough Nahanagan to your left. Every junction is signposted with the St Kevin's Way trail icon. Don't forget to look back down the valley along here to enjoy the incredible views.

At approx. 15.4km you'll reach the power station road, where you can cross over to rejoin the trail which leads you back up the car park.

Sorrel Hill

Sorrel Hill is in the Wicklow Mountains National Park. This trail follows an ancient mass path to the summit of Sorrel Hill. Mass paths are walkways linking rural communities with their local places of worship. Many Irish mass paths date from penal times (1695–1849), when the track would have led to a mass rock, where Catholic mass was celebrated in secret. Many mass paths from this time would cross streams and rivers so as to hide footprints and maintain the secrecy of the mass rock location from the authorities.

On this hike you will enjoy spectacular views of Poulaphouca Reservoir, more commonly known as Blessington Lakes. Dublin City Council and the Electricity Supply Board (ESB) acquired over 5,000 acres of land in the area to construct a dam and reservoir. In preparation for the flooding, 55 homes, 12 labourers' cottages and numerous farms, as well as roads and bridges, were destroyed. The filling of the reservoir commenced in March 1940, taking 18 months to reach full capacity.

What You Need to Know

OSI: 56
Height: 599.5m
Distance: 8km
Approx. time: 2.5–3 hours
Difficulty: moderate
Route type: out-and-back
Starting point: Church of Our Lady of Mount Carmel, Lacken, Blessington
Elevation: 400m
Parking: yes, 10–12 spaces, but avoid using the car park during mass times, opt for parking nearby instead
Fee: no
Dog friendly: no

Other Hikes in the Area

MORE TO EXPLORE

There is a shorter route from Ballynultagh Gap (approx. 1.1km up to summit via direct trail), which is a great sunrise or sunset option. There are about 8 to 10 spaces in this car park.

PIT STOPS

Visit
- Blessington Greenway
- Russborough House
- Seefin Passage Tomb

Eat
- Hollywood Café
- VDA Coffee, Blessington
- Enda's Grocers
- Brew Twenty One

The reservoir completely covered the townland of Ballinahown, known as the hidden village, as well as half of the townland of Lacken.

This trail is a favourite for those looking for hikes on the Kildare side of Wicklow and it offers a great sunrise location.

> **Note:** A large section of this trail is marked, until the open mountain. Look out for small white 'mass path' signage with green arrows. These can be on trees and are sometimes hard to see.

THE TRAIL

From the car park, walk back up the road you came down. Almost immediately to your right you will see a gap in the stone wall, steps and a small sign for the 'mass path'. Walk up the steps and onto the narrow gravel trail.

You will then pass through a black metal gate onto the road, turn right following the 'mass path' sign, which is on the pole across the road.

Approx. 60m along the road, turn left where you will see a blue boat flowerbed, and a 'mass path' sign. Pass through the wooden gate which says 'mass path' along with a 'no dogs' sign.

Head up the narrow trail, and from here follow the 'mass path' signposts.

You will pass through wooden gates (one of which is a swing gate).

At approx. 900m the trail runs up an

open grassy slope.

At approx. 1.1km from the car park, you get to a wooden stile: cross the stile and turn right following the sign for 'Lugnagun'.

Follow the narrow path up through the trees as it crosses over two fire roads (forest roads) following more signs for 'mass path' (the signs are very small so do keep a lookout for them).

At approx. 1.7km pass by another wooden stile and you will come out of the forest. There are a few trails splitting off here; turn right, following the trail as it runs alongside the forest line (the forest will be to your right-hand side).

At approx. 2.3km the forest to your right ends and the trail continues straight ahead and cuts through the open mountain. Here it is a distinct, grassy and boggy trail.

At approx. 3.3km the trail inclines for the final 700m ascent towards Sorrel Hill summit.

At approx. 4km you will reach the large summit cairn.

Return the way you came.

Glen Beach Cliff Walk

This trail shows off the Wicklow coastline at its finest. This area is within the Wicklow Head Special Protection Area, due to the presence of a population of kittiwake, although numerous species of birds breed in this area and will be evident as you hike, including the fulmar, shag, guillemot, herring gull, black guillemot, razorbill, peregrine falcon and raven. There are also sites of archaeological interest, including a rock shelter where prehistoric flints were found, the ruins of a lime kiln and a holy well. Of most interest, perhaps, are the grey seals at Lime Kiln Bay. They breed annually here from September to December and are best observed at a far distance. It is particularly important to keep dogs on a leash so as not to disturb the seals. The trail is rugged and best explored at off-peak times as it's quite narrow; the loop used to extend towards the lighthouse but in recent times it has been shortened due to private land access, so keep in mind that some of the online maps are incorrect for this route.

What You Need to Know

OSI: 56
Distance: 4km
Approx. time: 1 hour
Difficulty: moderate
Route type: lollipop circuit
Starting point: Glen Beach Cliff Walk car park, Wicklow (height restriction 2.1m)
Elevation: 100m
Parking: yes
Fee: no
Dog friendly: yes, on a leash

Other Hikes in the Area

Devil's Glen (p.97)

Note: This is a stunning trail to enjoy cliff views, wildlife and the sunrise. These cliffs are exposed so you have to be extremely cautious.

THE TRAIL

The trail is distinctive, it runs close to exposed cliffs and can get over grown in sections.

From the car park, follow the trail down towards Glen Strand Beach; this is a hard-surfaced trail with steps.

From the beach the rugged trail begins to the right, running adjacent to the water and cliff.

The sea will be on your left-hand side.

At approx. 1.2km the trail splits; you can continue straight where the trail runs through a gap in the rocks or turn left to loop around along the cliff to Ceann Bhride.

On the way out I recommend going left, as almost immediately along this section to your left you'll see a lovely viewpoint looking back along the cliffs and the sea arch.

Follow this trail around and at approx. 1.4km you'll reach Ceann Bhride point looking down onto the hidden beach, which is where the colony of seals will be at certain times of the year. Remember to keep your distance and stay out of sight of the seals.

Continue on the trail as it runs around the hidden beach (not going down to the beach itself).

At approx. 1.8km keep left as the trail splits.

At approx. 2.2km, just before the road, the trail loops back, and at approx. 400m, you will meet your original route to return to the car park.

PIT STOPS

Swim
- Glen Strand
- Magheramore Beach

Visit
- The Black Castle
- Travelahawk Beach
- Wicklow Historic Gaol
- Golden Arches viewpoint
- K2Alpacas
- Beyond the Trees Avondale

Eat
- Firehouse Bakery
- Le Marche
- Vital Health Café
- The Good Life Coffee Shop
- Nick's Coffee

Mount Leinster and Slieve Bawn

Ir. Stua Laighean, 'prince or warrior of Leinster'

Mount Leinster is the highest point in the Blackstairs Mountain Range, which forms the boundary between counties Carlow and Wexford. Some say that the mountain's Irish name, *Stua Laighean*, or prince/warrior of Leinster, comes from its imposing presence in the surrounding landscape, reminiscent of a protector standing guard over the province Surprisingly, given its name, it is not the highest point in Leinster: that honour goes to Lugnaquilla in Wicklow.

Unusually, due to the location of a large transmitter tower, there is an access road the whole way to the summit. The transmitter was one of the five original television transmitters erected in the early 1960s to broadcast the newly founded Raidió Teilifís Éireann (RTÉ). Today the transmitter broadcasts Saorview and eight FM radio stations to the south-east of Ireland. The old and new are combined at the summit, as alongside the transmitter you will also see a cairn. On the hike you will see the stone formation, known

What You Need to Know

OSI: 68
Height: 794m (Mount Leinster)
Distance: 8.2km
Approx. time: 2.5 hours
Difficulty: moderate
Route type: out-and-back
Starting point: Nine Stones car park
Elevation: 480m
Parking: yes, about 30 spaces
Fee: no
Dog friendly: yes, on a leash

Other Hikes in the Area

INCLUDED IN *THE HIKE LIFE* **(BOOK ONE)**
Blackstairs Mountain (p.133)

MORE TO EXPLORE
Mountain Leinster via Knockroe Hill for a longer adventurous trail (13.2km)

Leinster

> **PIT STOPS**
>
> **Swim**
> - Clashganny
>
> **Visit**
> - Clashganny Lock and Mass Rock
> - The Hot Box Sauna, Rosses Point
> - Silaire Woods
>
> **Eat**
> - Clashganny House
> - Brother Coffee, Bunclody
> - Sha-Roe Bistro, Clonegall

as the Nine Stones, although if you count them there are in fact ten! The origin of the Nine Stones is unknown – one legend connects the monument to nine shepherds who died on the mountain during a storm.

Mount Leinster has an infamous association with the wolf. It was here in 1786 that John Watson, a local landowner, killed the last wolf in Ireland, ending Ireland's ancient ties to *Mac Tíre*, the 'son of the countryside'.

I've included Mount Leinster and Slieve Bawn together, however you can hike them separately depending on the time you have.

Mount Leinster is a great one to tick off as a high point for both County Carlow and Wexford, and it's a lung buster with its continuous climb. It is also great for anyone who may need even terrain, as it is paved 90 to 95% of the way. The trail to Slieve Bawn is very short, but not marked. However, the well-worn trail is straightforward and gets you to the summit within 15 to 20 minutes. Slieve Bawn is an ideal hike if you are looking for a sunset viewpoint.

> **Note:** This trail is dog friendly, but there is a risk of this changing because of an increase in sheep attacks along this hike, due to irresponsible dog owners. Check online to see any recent updates, and keep your dog on a leash at all times!

THE TRAIL: MOUNT LEINSTER

From the car park, you will see a metal gate with grey pillars. Pass through the gate and onto the access road.

This trail is very straightforward following the access road as it steadily ascends the entire way up to the mast.

At approx. 2.7km, just before the mast, turn right where there is a grassy path leading to the summit marker. You will reach the summit marker at approx. 2.8km.

> **Note:** Make sure to explore the summit and its different vantage points. From here you get incredible views over to the Blackstairs Mountains and back down towards Slieve Bawn.

Return the way you came. This out-and-back is approx. 5.8km with approx. 400m elevation.

THE TRAIL: SLIEVE BAWN

Return back to the road, cross with caution, and on the other side you will see a mountain trail begin from the car park. It's a worn trail, visible through the grass.

Follow this trail as it rises up to the summit; from the car park to the summit marker it's approx. 1.2km.

Slieve Bawn summit offers amazing views back to the Blackstairs range and across to Croaghaun and Greenoge Mountains.

Return via the way you came; this out-and-back is approx. 2.4km with 80m elevation.

Raven Wood Nature Reserve
Ir. Dioghais, 'fortified height'

If you're looking for a trail that can offer you forests, water, sand and wildlife . . . look no further. It's a place your dog will love too. This walk paired with my below pit stop suggestions offers the perfect day out.

Raven Wood Nature Reserve was created in the 1930s to limit coastal erosion and protect an area to the west of the forest, known as the North Slob. The North Slob lands comprise of a sand dune system and grassy areas which are home to wild goose populations in the winter. On winter evenings, the wild geese fly out in formation at twilight which makes for a wonderful sight. The area is part of the Raven Nature Reserve, and the larger Wexford Wildfowl Reserve. The Raven's sand dunes have been forming since the 1600s; here flora and fauna have been identified that have disappeared elsewhere. The forest opens onto Curracloe Beach. Famous for its soft, fine sand, it stretches along 11km of coastline. The opening scenes of the Second World War movie, *Saving Private Ryan*, were filmed on the beach.

What You Need to Know
OSI: 77
Distance: 5.94km
Approx. time: 1.5-2 hours
Difficulty: easy
Route type: lollipop circuit
Starting point: Raven Wood Nature Reserve
Elevation: 53m
Parking: yes, about 65 car spaces and overflow car parks
Fee: no
Dog friendly: yes, on a leash

THE TRAIL

From the car park head towards the beach and trail head, passing by bins and sometimes a coffee van. The tarmac road ends and you'll see a trail for the beach to your left and the Raven Wood's loop trail to your right. There is signage about the trail here which is worth photographing to reference in case you find yourself confused later; it also highlights potential risks at high tide.

Following the trail to your right, very quickly you pass through a barrier and from here follow the red trail markers, which will guide you for the entire route.

The trail is hard surfaced, switching between gravel and dirt terrain. It can be waterlogged at certain times of the year.

When you return to your start point, it's worth following the trail to visit Curracloe Beach as the path down to the beach is stunning.

PIT STOPS

Swim
- Curracloe Beach

Visit
- The Surf Shack Ireland
- Blackwater Open Farm
- Wexford town
- Carrigfoyle Quarry

Eat
- The Trough
- The Clovelly

Portrane to Donabate Coastal Walk

This trail is perfect if you want a relaxing coastal walk, with lovely beaches and great views. This trail takes in the Donabate-Portrane Peninsula, north of Dublin City. The peninsula has a distinctive hammer-head shape, due to the large sand spits located at the mouths of both estuaries either side of the peninsula. The trail offers wonderful views of Howth and Lambay Island.

The turning point for this hike is a Martello tower, one of approximately 50 distinctive stone defensive towers built along the eastern coastline of Ireland. Martello towers were built across the British Empire in the 19th century, to defend against possible invasion by France, then under the rule of Napoleon I. Along the Dublin coastline alone, there are 26 towers within view of each other. The towers were named after the round fortress at Mortella, on the island of Corsica, which proved difficult for the British to capture and so they replicated its design. They misspelled the name of the original location however, and Mortella became Martello.

The official version of this trail is longer, as it includes a section on a road. I have removed this to make it a simple off-road

What You Need to Know

OSI: 43
Distance: 3.8km
Approx. time: 1 hour
Difficulty: easy
Route type: out-and-back
Starting point: Tower Bay car park, Portrane
Elevation: 10m
Parking: yes, about 80 spaces
Fee: no
Dog friendly: yes, on a leash

Other Hikes in the Area

INCLUDED IN *THE HIKE LIFE* (BOOK ONE)
Howth Cliff Walk (p.85)

out-and-back.

    Personally, I think the Portrane to Donabate coastal walk can be part of a perfect day out. Start with some lovely pastries and coffee, walk the trail, go for a sauna and dip, and finish the day with pizza by the sea. It doesn't get much more perfect than that!

THE TRAIL

From the car park follow the trail, which immediately splits in two.

> **Note:** The trail to the left is the old coastal path, which is on the cliff edge, and deemed unsafe and dangerous. It is not advised to take this trail. Take note of the danger signs here.

Follow the trail to the right. It is a tarmacked trail that runs on the inside of the old coastal path, separated by a small wall and fence.

At approx. 500m the trail cuts through a gap in a stone wall: there is a short rocky section here.

Continue to follow the tarmac trail.

At approx. 1.5km the trail narrows for a short section as it arrives at a red shelter.

Follow the trail as it turns right after the shelter. Continue to follow the trail as it runs parallel to Ladies Beach, where you get amazing views to Ireland's Eye, Howth and even the Sugarloaf.

> **Note:** While this section alongside the beach is beautiful, the trail gets narrow, and depending on the time of year, slightly overgrown, especially just as you approach Donabate.

At approx. 1.9km you reach the Martello tower and can enjoy the view of Donabate Beach.

This is an out-and-back route, so simply return the way you came.

PIT STOPS

Swim
- Tower Bay Beach, Portrane

Visit
- The Sea Sauna

Eat
- Doughbox Wood Fired Pizza
- An Bácús Beag (The Little Bakery)
- Triangle Coffee Co.
- Piper's Takeaway (for fish and chips)

Mullaghmeen

Ir. Mullach Mín, 'smooth summit'

Mullaghmeen is the highest point in Co. Westmeath, but at 258m it is the lowest of Ireland's County High Points. Mullaghmeen more than makes up for its stature with well-marked trails, lots of interesting history, great pit stops nearby and wonderful views over the Midlands from the top. Mullaghmeen Forest is managed by Coillte and is the largest planted beech forest in Ireland, and indeed Europe. The area was once farmland, part of an estate owned by Lord Gradwell. On the various trails you will see remnants of times past, including famine relief walls, a booley hut used by shepherds and families with summer grazing animals and flax pits, where the crop was harvested and prepared to make linen.

Mullaghmeen is well worth a visit at any time of year, but especially during bluebell season (April and May), when the forest is alive with the sight and scent of this beautiful flower.

What You Need to Know

OSI: 41
Height: 258m
Distance: 4.5km
Approx. time: 1 hour
Difficulty: easy-moderate
Route type: looped
Starting point: Mullaghmeen Forest, Co. Westmeath
Elevation: 180m
Parking: yes
Fee: no
Dog friendly: yes, on a leash

There are four marked trail loops at Mullaghmeen Forest:

- Yellow (1.4km)
- Red (3.5km)
- Blue (4.4km)
- White (8km)

> **Note:** This loop is really well-marked, just be sure to keep a lookout for the blue markers at each junction.

THE TRAIL

> **Note:** Take a picture of the information board at the start which you can refer to throughout the hike if needed.

From the car park, pass through the barrier on the left and follow the wide gravel forest road.

At approx. 200m at the first junction, keep straight following the blue arrows, then after 150m at the junction again keep straight, following the blue arrows.

At approx. 1.1km keep straight following the blue arrows.

At approx. 1.6km go left, following the blue arrows, and after 300m turn right to hike up towards Mullaghmeen high point.

> **Note:** The trail from here gets steep and narrow. At certain times of the year it can be overgrown.

At approx. 2.3km you reach a small cairn to your left-hand side; this is the highest point of Co. Westmeath.

Follow the trail as it continues along the top of Mullaghmeen and descends down

PIT STOPS

Swim
- Lough Lene
- Lough Owel Diving Boards

Visit
- Loughcrew Cairns
- Hill of Mael
- Tullynally Castle & Gardens
- Fore Abbey

Eat
- The Happy Cup Café, Oldcastle
- Barrel & Bean Café, Fore Distillery
- The Seven Wonders, Fore

along a narrow dirt trail.

Along this next section, you are on a narrow trail through the woods; there are also very steep descent sections. The terrain is mucky here too, which can make it difficult to get secure footing. You will need to concentrate during these sections!

At approx. 3.1km at the junction keep straight and follow the blue arrow.

At approx. 3.7km you will come to another junction; keep left here and continue to follow the blue arrows.

Finally, at approx. 3.9km, keep right and follow the blue arrows. You are now back on the wide forest trail.

At 4.4km you will return to the car park through the other barrier.

Leinster [141]

Munster

Cruach Mhárthain • Sauce Creek
Strickeen Mountain from Gap of Dunloe
Derrycunnihy Church to Lord Brandon's Cottage Mass Path
Bray Head, Valentia • Knocknadobar • Gleninchaquin Park
Hungry Hill • Three Castle Head • Knockomagh
Ardmore Cliff Walk • Nire Valley Trails • The Devil's Bit
Moylussa • Kilkee Cliff Walk and Loop Head • Abbey Hill

Cruach Mhárthain
(Croaghmarhin)

Ir. Cruach Mhárthain, 'stack of Márthain'

The trail offers great views of the Blasket Islands, an uninhabited group of islands, located about 2km off the Dingle Peninsula. These islands are the most westerly point in Europe. The Great Basket (An Blascaod Mór), the largest of the islands was inhabited until around 1954. The government, no longer in a position to guarantee the safety of the ageing population, relocated the community to the mainland. The island is perhaps most famous for being the birthplace of the Irish language literary icon Peig Sayers. The islands have become a popular tourist destination, with incredible cliffs, deserted villages, and wildlife, including a large seal colony, among the attractions. Each year a global competition to find a caretaker for Great Blasket Island from April to October attracts thousands of applications. The winners live on the Great Blasket, running the hostel and shop and documenting life on the island @greatblasketcaretakers.

This is one of the quickest (alas very steep) hikes in Kerry. It offers such greats views, and is one of my favourites when I'm in Dingle and want a good sunset spot.

What You Need to Know

OSI: 70
Height: 403m
Distance: 2km
Approx. time: 1 hour
Difficulty: moderate
Route type: out-and-back
Starting point: 52.141798, -10.425453, Cruach Mhárthain Glanmore, Kerry
Elevation: 225m
Parking: yes, but only 3-4 spaces
Fee: no
Dog friendly: yes, on a leash

THE TRAIL

The trail is short but very steep and unmarked. However, the path is very distinctive and worn, and it runs alongside a fence for the majority of the hike.

From the small car park follow the trail to the right-hand side of the large mast; it is a narrow trail through the grass.

At approx. 100m the trail passes through a small metal gate; continue following the

PIT STOPS

Swim
- Wine Strand

Visit
- Clogher Head
- Conor Pass drive
- The Blasket Centre
- Dingle Sea Safari
- Blasket Island Tours
- Outwest
- Páidi Ó Sé's pub
- Dunquin Pier
- Dunmore Head
- Coumeenoole Beach
- Slea Head Drive (Note: this is a one-way system in a clockwise direction through Ventry)

Eat
- My Boy Blue Dingle
- Nourish Café
- Seed and Soul
- Bean in Dingle
- The Hatch
- Pig and Leaf Coffee and Sandwiches
- The Fish Box / Flannery's Seafood Bar
- Doyle's Seafood Restaurant

trail as it runs alongside a fence.

At approx. 600m the trail passes through another small metal gate. Keep following the trail upwards.

The gradient is unforgiving so take breaks as needed along this section.

At approx. 1km you will reach the summit and can explore the top, where there are plenty of vantage points looking out towards the Blaskets, An Fear Marbh (the Sleeping Giant) and towards the Three Sisters and Ballyferriter village.

Return the way you came.

Other Hikes in the Area

Sauce Creek (p.149)

INCLUDED IN *THE HIKE LIFE* (BOOK ONE)
Mount Eagle (p.185)
Mount Brandon (p.179)

MORE TO EXPLORE
Ballydavid Head (5.7km)
Eask Tower (2.4km)
Ceann Sibeal (7km)
Gleannteenassig Forest Park
Annascaul Lake - Beenoskee (11km)

Sauce Creek

Ir. Faill an tSáis, 'cliff of the noose'

The Sauce Creek trail is at the northern end of the Mount Brandon range and takes its name from Sauce Creek Bay. The bay itself is 750m wide and surrounded by 400m-high cliffs, and very steep grassy slopes. In fact, these steep slopes were farmed by three local families until the early 1900s. It is hard to imagine once you see the gradient!

> **Note:** 'Sauce' is an anglicised version of the Irish *sás*, meaning 'noose'.

The bay itself was formed by strong northerly winds, driving waves into the shore. Over the years, the bay has continued to erode, resulting in landslides. The name Sauce – noose – refers to the fact that waves and currents make it very difficult to leave this cove by boat, especially in bad weather. Local fishermen used to say that if you went into the waters of the bay in bad weather you would never get out. The conditions at Sauce Bay led to some interesting finds during the Second World War, however, as the currents

What You Need to Know

OSI: 70
Distance: 7.6km
Approx. time: 2.5 hours
Difficulty: hard
Route type: out-and-back
Starting point: Sauce Creek Walkway, Teer, Co. Kerry
Elevation: 320m
Parking: yes, 4 spaces
Fee: no
Dog friendly: no

Recommended mountain leader: Piaras Kelly; kerryclimbing.ie

Other Hikes in the Area

Cruach Mhárthain (p.145)

INCLUDED IN *THE HIKE LIFE* (BOOK ONE)
Mount Brandon (p.179)
Mount Eagle (p.185)

MORE TO EXPLORE
Caherconree (6.5km)

washed up plenty of debris and wreckage from sunken ships, including barrels of rum and petrol.

There are lots of trail options, including Siúlóid An tSáis Loop, starting at Sauce Creek walkway or Brandon Point. If you have two cars you can do an A-to-B hike or do a longer out-and-back. Here I suggest an out-and-back with the most impressive views of Sauce Creek, which allows you plenty of time to enjoy Dingle.

> **Note:** This hike is not suitable in high winds, or poor visibility, as it runs alongside dangerous cliffs.

PIT STOPS

Swim
- Brandon Bay Beach
- Wild Water Adventures (for wild swimming tours)

Visit
- Brandon Point
- Conor Pass and Peddler's Lake
- Siopa An Phobail
- Maherees Beach
- Splash Sports Sea Safari
- Castlegregory
- Sandy Feet Farm

Eat
- Murphy's Bar Brandon

See Cruach Mhárthain (p.145) for more recommendations.

THE TRAIL

Out-and-back:
On this hike you will follow the signs for Siúlóid a tSáis (red arrows).

From the car park pass through the metal swing gate to the left-hand side of the farm gate.

Follow the wide stony trail as it gradually rises.

At approx. 2km the route turns left onto the narrow grassy, rocky and boggy trail, which is signposted 'Sauce Creek'.

Follow this trail and the red signs as it ascends gradually.

At approx. 2.8km the trail meets Sauce Creek and turns right to run along the cliff edge.

> **Note:** There are amazing views down to Sauce Creek all along this section. However, the cliffs are exposed along here so keep a safe distance from them.

Continue to follow the red signs and trail along here, enjoying the views off to your left-hand side, keeping a safe distance from the cliff edge. The cliffs are exposed until at about 3.6km when a fence begins.

The trail then begins to gradually descend towards Slieve Glass point. The trail is narrow, boggy and grassy with a fence to your left-hand side where you still get great views out to Sauce Creek.

At approx. 4.3km the arrow and trail turns right, away from Sauce Creek.

So far, these have been the best views of the creek so you can do an out-and-back and return the way you came. For A-to-B, continue following the waymarker arrows right.

A-to-B:
At approx. 4.3km the trail turns right (look out for the marker indicating a right turn).

The trail then begins to move away from the cliffs and sea views inland to run by Cnoc Duíléibhe and An Buaicín spot heights. The trail is boggy, before turning into a stoney trail and finally a grassy green road.

At approx. 7.4km the trail once again meets the cliffs and begins to descend to Brandon Point, passing a Second World War lookout post. The cliffs and a fence will be on your left-hand side.

At approx. 7.9km you'll pass over a stile and reach Brandon Point.

Loop:
If you want to do the loop, you continue on the road to loop back to your start point.

The full Siúlóid an tSáis loop is 13.6km, 370m elevation with a section of road; it is rated hard and will take approx. 4 hours.

Strickeen Mountain from Gap of Dunloe

Ir. Struicín, 'little peak'

Strickeen Mountain is located in Kerry and the renowned Gap of Dunloe. The name Dunloe comes from the Gaelic name *Dún Loich*, meaning 'fort' Loich. It is named for Loich, leader of the Fir Bolg, an ancient tribe from Irish mythology. The Gap of Dunloe is over two million years old, formed when a slow-moving glacier carved a mountain pass between the MacGillycuddy's Reeks and Purple Mountain, leaving huge boulders scattered all over the valley. One of these is known as the Turnpike, which forms a natural gateway on a narrow section of the pass. Close to the Turnpike is an old stone bridge known as the Wishing Bridge, where it is said your wishes can come true. The River Loe flows through the valley, linking five corrie lakes: Cocsaun Lough, Black Lake, Cushnavally Lake, Auger Lake, and Black Lough. Strikeen is also great for spotting sea eagles, kestrels and ravens.

This is a stunning, moderate hike, which gives you real bang for your buck! The

What You Need to Know

OSI: 78
Height: 440
Distance: 7.4km
Approx. time: 2.5–3 hours
Difficulty: moderate
Route type: out-and-back
Starting point: Kate Kearney's Cottage, Gap of Dunloe, Killarney
Elevation: 380m
Parking: yes, 70–80 spaces
Fee: no, however do go in and support Kate Kearney's
Dog friendly: no

Note: There is a small layby area for 3-4 cars at 'Strickeen Mountain Trail Head'; however, it is best to park at Kate Kearney's.

views along this trail down towards the Gap of Dunloe are some of my favourites, and the summit, although slightly lower than the towering peaks nearby, also offers great panoramic views. If you liked Torc Mountain from my first book you will really enjoy this hike.

PIT STOPS

Visit

- O'Sullivan's Cascade, Tomies Woods
- Wishing Bridge
- Gap of Dunloe
- Ross Castle and Library Point
- Innisfallen Island

Eat

- Heather Café
- The Dunloe Hotel & Gardens
- LUNA coffee + Wine, Killarney
- Hilliard's Killarney
- Café du Parc
- Good Boy Specialty Coffee Roasters
- J.M. Reidy's, Killarney
- The Coffee pot Café (for cake!)
- The Europe Hotel & Resort
- Emilie's, Killorglin
- Kingdom 1795, Killorglin
- Leaf & Larder Delicatessen and Bakery

See Derrycunnihy Church to Lord Brandon's Cottage Mass Path (p.161) for more recommendation around Killarney.

Other Hikes in the Area

Derrycunnihy Church to Lord Brandon's Cottage Mass Path (p.161)

INCLUDED IN *THE HIKE LIFE* (BOOK ONE)
Torc Waterfall and Mountain (p.195)
Mangerton Mountain Loop (p.199)
Carrauntoohil (p.189)

THE TRAIL

From Kate Kearney's, walk up the road towards the Gap of Dunloe. As you go, be mindful of traffic.

At approx. 750m the trail for Strickeen will be to your right, up a narrow, rocky trail. There is an information board here and a metal swing gate to pass through.

From this point there's a rocky, grassy path that steadily zigzags up the mountainside.

The views all along this section are amazing; be sure to look back down towards Purple Mountain and the Gap of Dunloe.

At approx. 3.1km, just as the rocky trail ends (there an 'end of trail' sign here), turn right towards Strickeen summit; the trail along here is grassy and boggy. As you get closer to the summit the terrain turns rocky.

At approx. 3.7km you will reach Strickeen summit, which is marked by three small cairns.

Take in the views from the summit out to Lough Leane, Killarney, and back to the MacGillycuddy's Reeks.

Return the way you came.

Derrycunnihy Church to Lord Brandon's Cottage Mass Path

What You Need to Know

OSI: 78
Distance: 10.6km
Approx. time: 3 hours
Difficulty: moderate
Route type: out-and-back (or A-to-B if you get the boat back)
Starting point: Derrycunnihy Church (closed) layby car park
Elevation: 200m
Parking: yes, 10 spaces
Fee: no
Dog friendly: yes, on a leash

Other Hikes in the Area

Strickeen Mountain from Gap of Dunloe (p.155)
Gleninchaquin Park (p.173)
Knocknadobar (p.169)
Bray Head, Valentia (p.165)

INCLUDED IN *THE HIKE LIFE* (BOOK ONE)
Torc Waterfall and Mountain (p.195)
Mangerton Mountain Loop (p.199)
Carrauntoohil (p.189)

I was introduced to this hike in the Killarney National Park by my friends in Kerry Climbing, and I immediately knew I had to include it in this book. Usually when I come to Killarney I am on a mission to take on some high summits, but this trail is equally as rewarding. It is a great hike for either a sunny or rainy day, although the waterfall is at its best in full flow, after the rain. Part of this trail is on the Kerry Way, a long-distance trail traversing the Iveragh Peninsula.

The first time I did this hike I was so fortunate to see white-tailed eagles soaring overhead. The reintroduction of these birds began in 2007 at the Killarney National Park, and continues to this day. I haven't seen them since, but you might if you keep an eye on the sky as you hike. I also got to see the herd of Old Irish goats living along the route. They are a real favourite of mine. The Old Irish goat is a native rare breed, unique to Ireland. They are especially important for their conservation grazing of gorse, which has been shown to reduce the risk of hillside fires.

The mid-point of this hike is Lord Brandon's Lodge, a café that is open in the summer months. You can pair this hike with a boat ride through the Upper Lake back to Killarney via Gap of Dunloe Traditional Boat Tours (they are dog friendly too). It's best to book any boat trips in advance.

This hike also offers wonderful views of the Black Valley, a remote valley at the southern end of MacGillycuddy's Reeks. The valley is so remote it was one of the last places in Ireland to be connected to electricity in 1976. Which might explain its name!

cross it, and in approx. 100m you'll see a narrow trail to your right which leads up to another waterfall view (approx. 180m). Return back to the junction. (This out-and-back section is approx 1km.)

Return to the trail, and continue, following signs for 'Kerry Way Black Valley'. From here it is approx. 3.2km following the wide, stony path, which meanders through the forest and then alongside the upper lake to Lord Brandon's Lodge.

At approx 5.3km you reach Lord Brandon's Lodge.

Return the way you came, or via the boat if you have booked it.

THE TRAIL

From the car park cross the road carefully where the trailhead begins. Look out for the sign that says 'Kerry Way'.

The trail is a narrow, rocky and muddy one down through the trees.

Follow this trail as it meanders down through the forest.

At approx. 1.1km, you will arrive at a junction.

> **Note:** This next part of the trail is a short out-and-back section to see the waterfall, so you will be coming back to this junction to continue on the trail.

At the junction, turn right for N71 (this is signposted). Now, follow this wide stony path until just before the wooden bridge where you need to turn left down a narrow trail (20m) to see the falls.

You can then return up to the bridge,

PIT STOPS

Swim
- Dundag Beach, Muckross

Visit
- Ladies' View viewpoint
- Owengariff River viewpoint
- Torc Waterfall
- Muckross Abbey
- Ross Castle
- Gap of Dunloe
- Lough Barfinnihy Viewpoints

Eat
- The Strawberry Field
- Café du Parc
- Hilliard's Killarney
- Good Boy Specialty Coffee Roasters
- LUNA coffee + wine
- J.M. Reidy's, Killarney

Bray Head
Valentia
Ir. Valentia, Béal Inse, 'approach to the island'

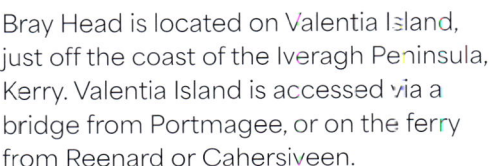

Bray Head is located on Valentia Island, just off the coast of the Iveragh Peninsula, Kerry. Valentia Island is accessed via a bridge from Portmagee, or on the ferry from Reenard or Cahersiveen.

> **Note:** This car park offers great views with no height restriction and the Bray Head walk offers wonderful views of the Skelligs, Kerry Cliffs and Puffin Island.

Puffin Island is small island between Valentia and Portmagee. This Irish Wild Bird Reserve is home to thousands of puffins, Manx shearwaters, and storm petrels. Only those conducting research on the birds can visit the island.

The extraordinary Skellig Islands are a UNESCO world heritage site and are among the most spectacular medieval monastic sites in the world. The distinctive shard-like profile juts out of the water, surrounded by jagged cliffs and huge crashing waves. If you are lucky enough to visit Skellig Michael you will get to climb a

What You Need to Know
OSI: 83
Height: 239m
Distance: 5km
Approx. time: 1.5-2 hours
Difficulty: moderate
Route type: lollipop circuit
Starting point: Bray Head car park
Elevation: 225m
Parking: yes
Fee: €2 cash (parking meter on site)
Dog friendly: yes, on a leash

Other Hikes in the Area
Knocknadobar (p.169)

1,000-year-old stone staircase comprising of 500 steps. There are also stone beehive huts where the monks lived and prayed, as well as oratories, a cemetery, stone crosses, holy wells and the Church of St Michael. Skellig Michael was used as a location for two Star Wars movies: *The Force Awakens* and *The Last Jedi*. If I am in this area, a landing or eco tour of the Skelligs is my top activity. They've been my favourite Irish experience to date: whether it is a sunshine or cloudy day, they are magnificent.

On the Bray Head you will also see an abandoned signal tower from the Napoleonic War and you can also make out the remains of a large 'EIRE' sign, used by fighter pilots in the Second World War to identify this land as Ireland.

> **Note:** Not suitable for those uncomfortable with heights. A lot of the trail runs alongside exposed cliff, so avoid in bad weather or high wind gusts. Dogs must be fully controlled due to livestock and the cliff-edge nature of this hike.

PIT STOPS

Swim
- Glanleam Beach

Visit
- Skelllig Islands during puffin season (end of May-June-July)
- Geokaun Cliffs (€6 per car)
- The Valentia Island Tetrapod Footprints
- Kerry Cliffs (€5 per person)
- St. Finan's Bay
- Valentia Island Lighthouse

Eat
- The Watch House
- The Moorings Guesthouse & Seafood Restaurant @ The Bridge Bar
- The Pier
- Driftwood Surf Café
- An Bothán

THE TRAIL

From the car park, turn left following the wide gravel path.

You'll come to a gate with a stile to the right side; you'll also see a Bray Head Tower walk marker.

Pass over the stile and follow this wide, stony trail as it gradually leads to the signal tower.

At approx. 2.2km you will reach Bray Head Signal Tower.

From here, take time to enjoy the views. Bear in mind you are beside exposed cliffs and caution is important.

The trail from here is not as distinctive or marked.

To continue on the loop, follow the vague grassy trail as it ascends up along the cliffs. The cliff edge will be to your left-hand side: there is no barrier or fence, so caution is required. The views along this section are outstanding so make sure to take time to stop and turn around to look back down towards the Signal Tower.

At approx. 3km you'll reach Bray Head point (293m).

From here the vague trail then begins to loop back, gradually descending towards your original trail along a narrow, boggy and rocky path.

At approx. 4km you'll meet your original trail, turn left to return back to your start point.

Note: If it's been raining you may be better off doing an out-and-back to Bray Head Tower as the descending section of the loop can become waterlogged and muddy in wet conditions.

Knocknadobar

Ir. Cnoc na dTobar, 'hill of the wells'

Knocknadobar is one of three important sacred sites in Kerry, along with Mount Brandon and Skellig Michíl. Incidentally, all three are in sight of each other. Knocknadobar's impressive profile rises majestically out of Dingle Bay on the Iveragh Peninsula. The mountain is associated with St Fursey, a 6th century saint. At the start of the trail, you will see St Fursey's Well, which is known for its healing properties, especially for eye problems. In 1885 a local priest built 14 stations of the cross linking the Holy Well and the summit.

Knocknadobar has been a site of pilgrimage since pre-Christian times, especially for the festival of Lughnasa. This continues to the present day with pilgrims climbing the mountain on Reek Sunday in late July. It is also a designated Pilgrim Path of Ireland. In more recent history, you will see an 'ÉIRE' sign made out of rocks, dating from Second World War.

A fan favourite among The Hike Life community, the pilgrimage background means there are great markers, it offers incredible views and even though it stands at 690m the trail is a gradual ascent as long as you don't take any of these sneaky shortcuts I mention here!

What You Need to Know

OSI: 83
Height: 690m
Distance: 10.2km
Approx. time: 3.5-4 hours
Difficulty: hard
Route type: out-and-back
Starting point: Cnoc na dTobar Pilgrim Path, Killurly West, Cahersiveen Kerry
Elevation: 680m
Parking: yes, 12-14 spaces
Fee: honesty box, €3
Dog friendly: no

Recommended mountain leader: Piaras Kelly; kerryclimbing.ie

PIT STOPS

Swim
- Cuas Crom Beach
- Kells Old Pier

Visit
- Kerry Cliffs (pictured)
- Skelllig Islands during puffin season (end of May to July)
- Cahergal Stone Fort
- Leacanabuaile Ring Fort
- Ballycarbery Castle
- Kells Sheepdogs, Ring of Kerry
- Rossbeigh Mountain and Strand

Eat
- The Oratory Pizza and Wine Bar
- Bari Café & Deli
- Quinlan & Cooke Boutique Hotel & Seafood Restaurant

See Bray Head, Valentia (p.163) for more nearby.

THE TRAIL

Note: This hike is along a Pilgrim Path. The trail is vague in some parts; however, it is marked, so do keep an eye out for the various markers.

From the car park, follow the narrow trail up through the grass where you will immediately pass through a small metal gate.

From here follow the vaguely worn trail through the field (this is the only small section not marked). The terrain here is very rugged so keep an eye on the trail.

After approx. 200m you will come to a gate with a stile on the left side: cross over the stile.

From here the trail is marked by small white poles, white stations of the cross and, in some parts, red paint on rocks.

The trail is a combination of rocky, boggy and grassy terrains and has a consistent uphill ascent.

At approx. 1.1km you'll pass through another small metal gate, a swing gate, and continue to follow the marked trail.

From approx. 1.8km a series of zigzags begin on the trail. There are a number of shortcuts here which split the trail but it's best to keep to the designated trail to avoid further erosion (I say this as someone who accidentally took a shortcut before); and it doesn't cut off that much time as it's much steeper and therefore slower!

Along here there are great views down to Coonanna harbour, so take breaks to enjoy them.

At approx. 3.8km you're up on the shoulder of the mountain and you can get incredible views over the other side, but please note it is often extremely windy here.

Continue on the trail as it takes the final ascent to the summit; the original trail actually veers left to zigzag towards the peak but now there is a direct path up to the summit.

At approx. 4.8km you'll reach a very large white cross known as the 'Canon's Cross', which I think offers the best views out towards the Skelligs and Portmagee. Many people do an out-and-back from here as this is the end of the 14 stations of the cross.

The summit is another approx. 300m of a slight ascent up to where there is a summit marker.

The summit takes in the 360° views from the highest point over towards Dingle, where on a clear day you'll see the towering outline of Brandon and the Blaskets.

Other Hikes in the Area

Bray Head, Valentia (p.165)
Strickeen Mountain from Gap of Dunloe (p.155)

INCLUDED IN *THE HIKE LIFE* (BOOK ONE)
Carrauntoohil (p.189)
Mangerton Mountain Loop (p.199)
Torc Waterfall and Mountain (p.195)

Gleninchaquin Park

A hidden gem nestled in the kingdom that is County Kerry. Gleninchaquin Park is situated on the Béara Peninsula, and if you didn't know about it you would never simply come across it. The park is not only a hiking destination but also a sheep farm. It is located down a long, *very* narrow and winding road by Inchiquin Lough.

There are five marked trails in Gleninchaquin Park which offer everything from an easy stroll to a challenging hike. It is privately owned and so there is a fee for parking. They also require you to check in at the café and sign out when you leave to ensure you have finished your hike safely.

Gleninchaquin Park comprises over 600 hectares of mountain landscape. In 2005 the owner of the park, Donal Corkery, commissioned research into the natural and cultural environment of the area. Information on both of these studies can be found at the park, and on their website.

Local legend ties Gleninchaquin to one of the great 'epics' of Irish mythology, the *Táin Bó Cúailnge*, the Cattle Raid

What You Need to Know

OSI: 85
Distance: 4.3km
Approx. time: 1.5–2 hours
Difficulty: moderate–hard
Route type: looped
Starting point: Gleninchaquin Park
Elevation: 219m
Parking: yes
Fee: €7 adult, €6 senior/student €5 children €20 family (2 adults and 2 children)
Dog friendly: yes, on a leash

of Cooley. Next to Inchiquin Lough is a field known as Bull's Inch. It is said that when Queen Maeve, the warrior queen of Connaught, stole the Brown Bull of Cooley, she fled south to Kerry. The only place with a field large enough, or special enough, for the Brown Bull was in the valley of Gleninchaquin. There are also numerous ancient archeological sites in

PIT STOPS

Swim
- Glanmore Lake

Visit
- The Naked Sheep – Alpaca Trekking
- Derreen Garden (Gairdín Derreen)
- Healy Pass Drive
- Glanmore Lake View Point
- Cashelkeelty Stone Circles

Eat
- An Sibin Bar & Carvery
- Josie's Lakeview House
- Helen's Bar and Café
- Poffs, Kenmare
- PF McCarthy's Bar & Restaurant
- Sheen Falls Lodge
- Lime Tree Restaurant

Gleninchaquin Park, most notably several *Fulacht Fiadh*, or ancient cooking places, along the River Geartha, and of course the famine cottage.

There are four other marked trails, in addition to the 'Over-the-Waterfall Loop' described here. These are:

1. River Walk
2. Heritage Trail – another favourite of mine, which takes in the heritage site of the old famine cottage. It's shorter and offers some great picture opportunities of the waterfall and cottage. You can detour off the Waterfall Loop to take in some of the Heritage Trail.
3. Waterfall Upper Valley Walk
4. Boundaries Walk

THE TRAIL

There is a detailed information board at the map in the car park, which is handy to have a photo of.

The route is very well marked for its entirety with red (paint, arrows and red plastic). I'm giving a brief overview of the red loop combined with a short out-and-back to along the Heritage Walk, my favourite route in the park.

From the car park follow the 'red loop' arrow up along a tarmac road.

Follow the red 'waterfall' sign along here. At approx. 240m the trail passes through a farm gate, which should be closed behind you. Keep following the tarmac road. At approx. 500m the trail cuts

left across the grass (signposted 'red walk'). The route then crosses over a steel bridge (waterfall to your right), and from here the trail becomes a grassy stony path.

At approx. 700m you will pass through another farm gate, close this after you.

Follow the wide stony road as it gradually rises up. At approx. 980m you'll see a sign for 'Heritage Walk' to your right.

You can do a short out-and-back here to see the famine house, which I would recommend. At approx. 1.2km you'll be at the famine cottage where you can see amazing views towards the waterfall.

Return along the path you came on and once you're back on the red loop continue to follow the trail up to the right.

At approx. 1.6km the hard-surfaced trail ends and the trail turns left along a narrow rocky track. Now, the trail steadily rises and at approx. 1.9km it passes through a small gate. The trail then becomes narrower with some loose rock.

At approx. 2.1km the trail steeply climbs and at approx. 2.3km you will see spectacular views back down towards Cummeenadillure Lough. From here the trail levels out for a time along a stony loose-rock trail.

At approx. 2.5km the trail descends towards Cummeenaloughaun (another lake) and at approx. 2.9km it crosses over the top of the waterfall via a bridge: some amazing views here! The trail continues to be rocky and stony and at approx. 3km it goes over a stile. The trail begins its descent passing by a wooden swing gate and at approx. 3.2km you'll come to a steep set of stone steps to descend; there

Other Hikes in the Area
Hungry Hill (p.177)

INCLUDED IN *THE HIKE LIFE* (BOOK ONE)
Gougana Barra (p.203)

MORE TO EXPLORE
Knockboy (Cork's highest peak)

is a steel railing on one side for support.

At approx. 3.3km you pass through another farm gate: close it behind you. Then the trail turns into a grassy track that gradually runs down. Along here is a great picnic bench for a spot to stop.

At approx. 3.8km the trail turns right past a metal gate and into the forest. This is a gorgeous section of trail through the forest. It is a narrow rocky dirt track with some exposed tree roots that passes over several wooden bridges. The trail then comes out onto a tarmac road. Here you can turn right to return to the car park.

Hungry Hill
Ir. Cnoc Daod, 'hill of the tooth, teeth'

Hungry Hill is in the Caha Mountains, and is the highest peak in the Beara Peninsula with expansive views of Cape Clear Island and the Skelligs. Cape Clear Island, off the coast of Cork, is the most southerly inhabited point in Ireland. The island is a Gaeltacht (Irish-speaking) region, with a population of a little over one hundred people. Cape Clear is home to a bird observatory, and to many migratory birds, due to its climate, which is warmer than the mainland. The waters around Cape Clear are also home to seals, basking sharks and dolphins.

The Beara Peninsula is steeped in mythology. Legend has it, that the peninsula is the home of the goddess, Cailleach Bhéirre or the Hag of Beara. According to another tradition, the peninsula was named after a Spanish princess who married Eogán Mór, the head of the Eogánacht Munster dynasty. Hence the similarity between the names Beara and Iberia.

There are so many hikes on the Beara Peninsula, that picking between them was incredibly tough, and so I've left heaps of options near or around Beara Peninsula here.

What You Need to Know
OSI: 84
Height: 685m
Distance: 11.4km
Approx. time: 3.5-4 hours
Difficulty: very hard
Route type: out-and-back
Starting point: Don's Mountain Café, Healy Pass
Elevation: 740m
Parking: yes, approx. 3 spaces
Fee: no
Dog friendly: no

Recommended mountain leader:
Julie Reeves; juliereeveswalking@gmail.com
Sinéad Pollock-Orr; sineadpollockorr@gmail.com

Munster [177]

PIT STOPS

Swim
- Pooleen
- Zetland Pier
- Blue Pool and Deirdre's Lookout

Visit
- Garinish Island (a must!)
- Glengarriff Nature Reserve
- Eyeries (for its colourful houses)
- Allihies Copper Mine Museum
- Bere Island
- Dursey Island
- Drive Caha Pass and Healy Pass
- Glanmore Lake

Eat
- Dzogchen Beara Café
- Beara Necessities, Eyeries

In Castletownbere
- Catcha Coffee
- Breen's Lobster Bar
- The Curiosities Emporium

In Allihies
- Beara Barista
- Plenty of great pubs!

In Glengarriff
- Caha Coffee
- Eccles Hotel & Spa
- La Crêperie Gourmande
- Artisan Wood Fired Pizza

See Gleninchaquin Park (p.173) for more recommendations.

Hungry Hill is a hike for experienced hikers only; don't let 'hill' in the name mislead as you this is anything but. It's a beast of a climb and one of the hardest in these Hike Life books. However, you are rewarded with incredible views from islands to lakes and layer upon layers of mountain peaks near and far.

> **Note:** If you are from the area why not join a local hiking club like the Cork Hillwalkers or the Cork Backpackers Hillwalking Club who often take on some of the peaks I've mentioned below.

There are many routes up Hungry Hill: I prefer from Healy's Pass as it's an incredible scenic hike if you love challenging terrain and have navigational skills. It also takes you up one of Irelands most scenic drives as your start point.

Other Hikes in the Area

MORE TO EXPLORE

Dunboy Castle Loop (easy)
Pulleen Loop (easy)
Dursey Island Loop (cable car across)
Bere Lighthouse Loop (boat across)
Cumeengeera Horshoe Loop (very hard)
Knockboy (Cork's highest peak)
Knockoura (6.3km)
Beara Way (long distance trail)

Note: There is a shorter route from the west side (5.5km with 650m). This shorter route often comes up when you search "trails for hungry hil ", it is an extremely steep challenging route. I mention this route as I want to stress parking here is very limited here with only two spots in a lay by, if you go this way, Please do not block the houses or driveways at this cul-de-sac, as unfortunately such behaviour has happened here before which is really unfair on the locals.

THE TRAIL

Note: You will NOT be able to do this hike without navigational tools, as the lack of trails or signage and terrain make it difficult and dangerous to traverse. Due to the location, clouds can roll in from the sea very quickly and result in poor visibility. The below is a general overview of the route not a replacement for navigation.

This route's terrain is very boggy for the majority of the hike and every time you'll do this hike your distance will be slightly different there is a lot of zig zagging with no clear trail.

From the small car park at Doris Mountain Café, walk down the road (south side of Healy Pass), at approx. 200m the route turns up right to leave the road.

From here there are no trail or markers, and it is immediately steep and boggy.

At approx. 2.2km the route reaches Coombane peak at 510m. Some people like to do an out-and-back to here as it does give incredible views over to Agridole Mountain, down onto Healy Pass and Glanmore Lake.

To continue, the route crosses towards Derryclancy at 607m, ascending gradually where the terrain gets rocky with some sections where the trail is worn.

At approx. 3.6km you met Derryclancy summit, the route then begins to descend towards Hungry Hill along

a grassy, boggy and along exposed stone. Along the col (the dip between Derryclany and Hungry Hill), you get amazing views down to Coomadayallig Lake on your left-hand side.

The final ascent (on the way out) begins along the north side of Hungry Hill, this is the steepest section of this hike and having some form of navigation is very important here as there are steep drops along ether side. The route meets Hungry Hill summit marker and cairn at approx. 5.7km. There is a nearby spot height of 667m south of Hungry Hill which is nice to hike across to marked by a cairn giving great views out over Bere island and down towards Coomarkane Lake. When exploring the summit area be cautious that there are sheer drops, enjoy the views safely.

Return the way you came.

Three Castle Head
Ir: Ceann na dTrí Chaisleán/Dún Locha

The Three Castle Head trail is close to Ireland's most southwesterly point, Mizen Head, on the Mizen Peninsula. It is also the location of Dunlough Castle, one of the oldest castles in the south of Ireland. While the current structure dates from the 15th century, the original castle was constructed in 1207, and before that it was the site of a Bronze Age fort. The castle consists of three towers connected by a curtain wall, that extends from the cliffs to the lake. Although now ruins, the castle and its location are awe inspiring. There are some dark tales associated with Dunlough Castle and Three Castle Head. It is said that the O'Donohues, the last family to live there, all died tragically, and to this day a drop of blood falls into the lake from the smallest of the towers every day. This part of West Cork was also a centre of copper mining, and you will see signs of the mines as you drive in the area, most notably the Dhurode Copper Mine.

This hike is on private land and the owners have a few rules as it is a working farm and an area of conservation. These

What You Need to Know
OSI: 88
Distance: 4km
Approx. time: 1-1.5 hours
Difficulty: easy
Route type: out-and-back
Starting point: parking for Dunlough Fort
Elevation: 200m
Parking: yes, about 25-30 spaces
Fee: yes. July through August: €3 per person with U12s free (card accepted); the rest of the year it's an honesty box (cash)
Dog friendly: no

Other Hikes in the Area
Knockomagh (p.187)
INCLUDED IN *THE HIKE LIFE* (BOOK ONE)
Sheep's Head Lighthouse Loop (p.207)
Gougane Barra (p.203)

include: no dogs, drones, fishing, swimming, camping, bikes or commercial tours (without consent). Check their website at threecastlehead.ie. Here you can look at the trail options, book into their hideaway for the night and – fun fact! – you can get married at the castle.

This is one of my favourite Munster hikes to bring friends to because for such a short hike it packs in so many elements. A historic castle on a cliff with stunning lakes: it's a hike to wow!

I've included my favourite pit stops for this trip. Please ensure you give a full day in this part of Cork as there are so many amazing beaches and eateries. I hope you enjoy the best day out.

The walk is closed from 7 January to 31 March every year to give the land a break from visitors.

PIT STOPS

Swim
- Galley Cove
- Canty's Cove
- Ballyrisode Beach
- The Dog Hole, Schull
- Toormore Bay Beach
- Lackenakea Bay Beach
- Barleycove Beach (lifeguards can be here at weekends during summer)

Visit
- Altar Wedge Tomb
- Floating Walkway, Barleycove
- Mizen Head (entry fee)
- Fastnet Rock lighthouse tour
- Cape Clear Island

Eat
- Nottage Bar & Restaurant
- O'Sullivans Bar, Crookhaven
- Restaurant Chestnut, West Cork
- Oasis Arts Café
- Artichoke, Ballydehob
- Hudsons Wholefoods
- Budd's Restaurant & Rosie's Bar, Ballydehob
- The Perch, Schull
- FED @Schull Street kitchen

THE TRAIL

The trail is well-marked with 'Castle' and black arrows on white and from the castle itself you can meander up to a small cairn which is what I have described below.

You can add on distance by exploring around the castle and Dun Lough and usually I do anything between 4km and 6.5km depending on how I choose to take in different angles of the lough and castle.

The owners do a great job in maintaining the area and ensuring that there is fencing around the cliff, so they ask people not to jump over the fence and to be mindful of the places where the cliffs are exposed and to stay clear of danger.

From the car park, follow the tarmac road leading from the car park towards the house.

At approx. 150m follow the 'castle' sign off the road onto a grassy track.

This part of the route runs across fields on a worn grassy track.

At approx. 330m you'll pass through a small metal gate (this is where the honesty box is).

The trail from here turns right to go up alongside a fence (the fence is to your right).

This is all marked.

At approx. 570m you pass through another small metal gate.

From here the trail gets slightly wider and is a grassy stony path that gradually works its way towards the cliffs.

At approx. 1km the trail meets a fence and the cliffs; here the trail turns right and begins to steeply rise along a stony boggy trail. The fence will be to your left-hand side.

At approx. 1.3km you'll get your first view of the castle and the trail begins to descend towards it while remaining by the fence.

At approx. 1.5km you'll reach a small metal gate to pass through, following along the stony narrow trail and passing through a gap in the stone wall; now the castle will be to your right-hand side.

From here you can continue up along the grassy trail ascending to the small cairn at approx. 1.8km which overlooks Dun Lough and a smaller unnamed lake, with panoramic views across to Sheep Head, Mizen, Dunmanus Bay and out to sea.

This is a great place to explore along the visible grassy trails, being mindful that you are near cliffs.

Return the way you came.

Knockomagh

Ir. Loch Oighinn, 'lake of the cauldron'

What You Need to Know

OSI: 89
Height: 197m
Distance: 4km
Approx. time: 1 hour
Difficulty: moderate
Route type: out-and-back
Starting point: Lough Hyne Nature Reserve, Skibereen, Cork
Elevation: 178m
Parking: yes, and can be busy during peak times
Fee: no
Dog friendly: yes, on a leash

Note: This is a short trail but very steep in sections, both to ascend and descend.

Lough Hyne is one of my favourite spots in Cork. It is a truly unique place. A sea lough, it is Ireland's first Marine Nature Reserve. The lake is fed by tidal currents from the Atlantic pushing up through Barloge Creek and into the lake over the 'rapids'. The lake's highly oxygenated and warm water sustains a wide variety of plants and animals not found anywhere else in Ireland. I have visited the area often over the years, particularly for this trail, but also for the Atlantic Sea Kayaking tours. A must-do activity is night kayaking on Lough Hyne, where you can experience the magic of bioluminescence, the luminous phosphorescence creating the effect of twinkling stars in the water.

Swimming is not promoted in Lough Hyne to help combat the impact on the lake of overuse, but there are plenty of other wild dipping spots nearby.

The island in the centre of the lake is known as Castle Island, as it contains the ruins of Cloghan Castle, a fortress of the O'Driscoll clan, who are synonymous with this part of West Cork.

Stone walls are evident on the sloping sides of Lough Hyne. These were built as part of the famine relief work scheme, whereby the government employed the poor of Ireland to complete various public projects during the Great Hunger. The wages paid were very low, often late and insufficient to protect the population of West Cork from starvation.

PIT STOPS

Swim
- Tragumna Beach
- Dromadoon Pier

Visit
- Sunrise Sauna, Tragumna
- Barlogue Pier
- Atlantic Sea Kayaking, Lough Hyne
- Baltimore Beacon
- Fastnet Rock Lighthouse tours
- Sherkan Island
- Toe Head
- Sky Garden, Liss Ard Estate
- Cré Pottery Studio

Eat
- Dede at the Customs House, Baltimore
- The Algiers
- Rolf's Country House, Baltimore
- O'Neill Coffee Roasters
- Kalbo's Café
- Judy's Falafel, Skibereen
- An Sibín, Cork

Note: You can hike Knockomagh from the west side, the opposite side to Lough Hyne, if you prefer a less busy trail.

THE TRAIL

From the car park walk towards Knockomagh Wood. Along this road you will see a purple trailhead sign saying 'Knockomagh Summit 2km' – this is your start point. The trail is very easy to follow as it is the only trail leading upward to the summit and viewpoint.

This trail is immediately steep; it's a narrow forest dirt track that is rocky with some exposed tree roots and steps. The trail zigzags up. Be sure to take some breaks if you need to, as the gradient is strenuous.

At approx. 1.5km the trail splits: to the left is out towards the viewpoint, where a rocky narrow trail leads to an incredible vantage point overlooking Lough Hyne at approx. 1.7km.

From here, if you want to visit the summit, you can return back to the split in the trail then turn left to follow the narrow trail up to the Knockomagh spot height. Note that there is no marker for this summit and this section is very overgrown.

This is an out-and-back route, so return the way you came, taking care on the steep descent.

> **Note:** This trail can be especially difficult after rainfall.

Ardmore Cliff Walk

Ir. Aird Mhór, 'great height'

The walk follows a marked cliff-top trail with many points of interest. At the beginning of the cliff walk, you will come across St Declan's Well and Church. St Declan founded a seminary in Ardmore in the 5th century. The holy well was a place of baptism for early Christians, as well as a place of pilgrimage for hundreds of years. To this day, on 24 July each year, the feast day of St Declan, a 'Pattern' celebration is held in Ardmore with many pilgrims visiting the site.

The hike also passes an old coastguard station, which is now a private home, and a shipwreck known as the *Sampson*, which ran aground in 1988. There are also two lookout towers, one built in the 1860s during the Napoleonic Wars, and one during Second World War. Most impressive is the 29m-high round tower, at St Declan's ecclesiastical site. You will also find an oratory and the ruins of the cathedral adjacent to the tower.

Ardmore Cliff Walk is somewhere I grew up visiting. As soon as there was

What You Need to Know

OSI: 82
Distance: 4.1km
Approx. time: 1 hour
Difficulty: easy (marked route)
Route type: looped
Starting point: Ardmore town
Elevation: 85m
Parking: yes, on-street parking
Fee: yes, on-street parking meter
Dog friendly: yes, on a leash

Other Hikes in the Area

INCLUDED IN *THE HIKE LIFE* (BOOK ONE)
Dunmore East Cliff Walk (p.165)

MORE TO EXPLORE
Knockadoon Cliff Walk (7.8km)

a glimmer of sunshine, we escaped to Ardmore. As a child I was always captivated by the shipwreck of the *Sampson*, and it still holds a special fascination for children, including my nephews.

> **Public transport:** Buses from Dungarvan and Youghal (service 361). Youghal and Dungarvan are accessible by bus from Waterford and Cork.

PIT STOPS

Swim
- Goat Island

Visit
- Goat Island
- Ardmore Open Farm and Mini Zoo
- Ardmore Farmers Market (Sundays only)
- The Hot Pod, mobile sauna

Eat
- Whitehorses Restaurant
- The Garden Kitchen Café
- Cliff House Hotel

THE TRAIL

This hike is marked entirely with red arrow 'Cliff Walk Ardmore' waymarkers.

From the roundabout at the top of Main Street walk up the cliff road. This is a steep tarmac road; be careful of vehicles.

At approx. 600m from the roundabout, you will pass the Cliff House Hotel, which will be on your left. Continue walking past the hotel, and after approx. 100m a trail begins, which is signposted for 'St Declan's Hermitage'.

Take this narrow, hard-surfaced gravel trail. At approx. 700m you will pass by St Declan's Well and Church ruins. The trail continues along a narrow hard-surfaced track with a set of steps; the cliffs will be to your left-hand side, protected mostly by a fence along this section.

At approx. 1.8km you get to the lookout hut, information boards and a great view down at the shipwreck and of course across to the Watch Tower. Continue on the trail following the arrows right, along the gravel trail, passing by some benches where you can enjoy the views and Fr. O'Donnells Well. Note some sections along here are not fenced.

At 2.8km the trail passes by a gate and out onto a minor road. At approx. 3.2km you come to a junction, turn left and be mindful that this can be a busy road.

Follow the road down past Ardmore Tower, keeping an eye out for the markers.

At approx. 3.8km you'll arrive back

down onto Main Street, turn right following the signs for 'St Declan's Way' to walk up the Main Street and back to the roundabout where you began.

Nire Valley Trails

The Nire Valley comprises the western lower slopes of the Comeragh Mountains and is a treasure trove of coums and lakes. Visible from the trail is the Gap, a natural pass in the Comeragh Mountains, known locally as Bóithrín na Sochraide (the Funeral Road). Before 1862 there was no parish church in the Nire, and this meant bringing the dead across the Gap, for burial in the neighbouring village of Rathgormack.

Close to the Gap, you will see Coumlara, a hollow with no lake: this is one of the Comeragh's best examples of a dry coum. Also on the trail, you will see the Sgilloges, two of the Nire Valley's six lakes. The waterfall cascading in the first lake is known as Bean Píobra which means 'Woman with the Pipe', as when the wind blows from the southwest and the water is blown back over the waterfall, from a distance it looks like smoke rising.

I love hiking in the Nire Valley and the Comeraghs: they really are hidden gems. There are so many trail options here. The Sgilloges Walk (blue marked trail, out-and-back, 4km), Coumduala Loop (purple marked trail, 9km), Coumlara Loop (red marked trail 6.5km), the Gap Walk (green marked trail, out-and-back, 6km), plus Knockanaffrin summit and the

What You Need to Know

OSI: 75
Distance: 7.4km
Approx. time: 3 hours
Difficulty: moderate-hard
Route type: looped
Starting point: Nire Valley car park, Knockanaffrin, Waterford
Elevation: 460m
Parking: yes, 15-20 spaces
Fee: no
Dog friendly: no

Recommended mountain leader: Julie Reeves; juliereeveswalking@gmail.com

nearby Lough Mohra trail. I particularly enjoy doing the Sgillogues Walk, paired with the Coumduala Loop.

THE TRAIL

> **Note:** There is a great information board with a map at the start, which I would recommend taking a picture of for the trail options. Navigation is required for this area. Even though there are waymarkers they can be far apart in certain sections.

From the information board, the trail starts to the left along a distinctive steep and narrow grassy and rocky track; at approx. 470m the trails meet at a metal swing gate.

For the 'purple' Coumduala loop, don't pass through the metal swing gate. Instead the trail runs up along the fence on a grassy, rocky and boggy track. The fence will be on your right-hand side all along this section. The gradient along this section is steep with a section in the middle where it comes to a plateau (giving your legs a bit of a break).

> **Note:** From the fence you can turn left for Knockanaffrin and Knocksheegowna summits, another great hike in the Nire Valley for experienced hikers.

At approx. 2.2km the trail meets a fence; to your right there is a stile to pass over. Now you are directly above

Other Hikes in the Area

INCLUDED IN *THE HIKE LIFE* (BOOK ONE)
Coumshingaun Loop (p.159)
Slievenamon Loop (p.155)

Coumduala Lough and walking along exposed sheer drops to your left-hand side: caution is required. The trail along here is a distinct and narrow boggy track.

The trail levels out before descending towards the gap; be aware that some sections here are steep.

At approx. 3.5km you'll reach the gap, which I always think is a nice spot to have a break.

Continue along the the fence. At

approx. 3.6km you'll see a marker pole to your left by the fence and a vague grassy trail to your right; here is where you leave the fence along a vague grassy track.

The trail becomes distinctive again as it cuts along the side of the Carrignagower, which will be to your left-hand side.

The section of trail is very narrow with parts where you may need to use your hands to get over large rocks. There are also some footbridges and a section where there will be a fence running along the right-hand side of the trail. At approx. 5.5km, follow the blue markers trail to your left leading towards Sgilloge Loughs. Here the trail is narrow, rocky and boggy. After approx. 600m, you reach the first lough. This section is an out-and-back part of the route.

PIT STOPS

Visit
- Suir Blueway (Blueway at Kilsheelan)
- Mahon Falls
- Carey's Castle
- Lough Mohra

Eat
- Fetch Coffee, Clonmel
- Hanora's Cottage, Nire Valley

Returning back onto the Coumduala Loop, continue left following the trail. The trail along here dips in and out of being visible along a grassy, boggy track with a short section of boardwalk. At approx. 6.3km the trail crosses over a bridge, and the terrain becomes rocky for a short time. Continue following the trail and its blue arrows, as it turns into a stone and grassy roadway leading back to the car park.

The Devil's Bit

Ir. Bearnán Éile, 'little gapped hill of Éile'

What You Need to Know

OSI: 59
Distance: 2.4km
Approx. time: 1.5 hours
Difficulty: moderate
Route type: out-and-back
Starting point: Devil's Bit Hiking Trail
Elevation: 190m
Parking: yes
Fee: no
Dog friendly: yes, on a leash

Other Hikes in the Area

Moylussa (p.205)

INCLUDED IN *THE HIKE LIFE* (BOOK ONE)
Galtymore (p.147)
Slievenamon (p.155)

PIT STOPS

Swim
- Lough Derg, Ballycuggeran Beach, Twomilegate

Visit
- Lough Derg Blueway
- Rock of Cashel
- Birr Castle Demesne

Eat
- One19 Coffee House
- The Cottage Loughmore
- E53 Coffee House
- Bush & Briar Coffee
- Sos Beag Coffee
- The Green Sheep Café
- Mitchel House

The Devil's Bit, with its noticeable gap in its upper slopes, gives the mountain its name. Legend has it that the Devil took a bite out of the mountain, creating the gap. The Devil broke his teeth taking the bite, spitting out the rock, and creating the Rock of Cashel where it now stands. The linking of these two iconic Tipperary sites provides for a good story, which is what made me love this trail so much growing up. However, geology tells us that the Devil's Bit is entirely sandstone, while the Rock of Cashel is limestone.

In 1789, the 8th century manuscript, *The Book of Dimma*, was supposedly discovered in a cave on the Devil's Bit. This priceless manuscript had been lost since the 16th century, although there is debate as to whether the manuscript was actually found there, as such a fragile antiquity could not have survived undamaged in such an exposed location for so long. *The Book of Dimma* is currently preserved at Trinity College in Dublin.

As with many mountains in Ireland, the Devil's Bit has been a site of pilgrimage since pagan times, climbed for the festival of Lughnasa to welcome the harvest season. This tradition continues into the present with locals ascending the Devil's Bit for a Pattern Day pilgrimage on Rock Sunday, in late July.

The Devil's Bit offers expansive views of other mountains, including the Knockmealdown, Comeragh, Galtee and Slievenamon mountains.

THE TRAIL

Note: There are great online maps for the loop when it's back open. It is marked, but the summit area can be hard to navigate with its steep drops.

From the car park pass through the gate, closing it behind you, onto the wide stony trail. Follow the purple arrow markers and at approx. 400m pass through a metal swing gate.
    At approx. 800m you come to a junction. Here you go straight across following the purple arrow.
    Follow this narrow trail as it rises sharply. At approx. 900m the trail turns left towards the summit along a very narrow trail with steps and large rocks; scrambling is required along this section. At approx. 1.2km you will reach the Devil's Bit pilgrim cross.

Note: At the above turn there is a narrow trail straight ahead that offers a more gradual trail up to the summit.

    There is a loop for this hike (4.2km marked by purple arrows). However, it was closed for tree felling for a large period of 2024. It is marked, so once it is back open it's a great option to make this trail longer along a lovely forest track.

Moylussa
Ir. Maigh Lusa

Moylussa, in the Slieve Bearnagh range is County Clare's tallest peak, and a County High Point, standing at an impressive 532m tall. Access to the mountain is via Ballycuggaran Wood, named after the O'Cuggarans, an important clan in the court of Brian Boru, a High King of Ireland. Legend has it that Moylussa itself was the home of the ancient warrior Fionn mac Cumhaill, who used the mountain as a lookout point to defend Ireland against invaders. Moylussa offers spectacular views of Lough Derg, the largest lake on the River Shannon, and the third largest lake on the Island of Ireland. Close by is the Ardnacrusha hydroelectric power plant, which when built in 1927, was the largest in the world.

The area of Moylussa, Killaloe, which is settled on the border of Tipperary and Clare is a stunning place to enjoy a weekend away.

What You Need to Know
OSI: 58
Height: 532m
Distance: 9.6km
Approx. time: 3-3.5 hours
Difficulty: moderate (due to the steepness)
Route type: out-and-back
Starting point: Ballycuggaran Forest car park
Elevation: 500m
Parking: yes, about 25 spaces, and there is more parking available down by Twomilegate
Fee: no
Dog friendly: yes, on a leash

PIT STOPS

Swim
- Twomilegate

Visit
- The WasherWoman pub (for live music)
- McKernan Woollen Mills
- Wilde Irish Chocolates (where you can build your own chocolate bar)

Eat
- The Wooden Spoon
- Derg House Café
- West Lake Coffee
- The Garden Café
- The Old Barracks Coffee Roastery

THE TRAIL

From the car park you'll see an information board with the trail info. I recommend taking a snap of this in case you need to refer back to it throughout your hike.

To the left of the sign is a wide forest trail. Passing through the barrier, follow the wide forest track as it gradually ascends, following the yellow and red markers.

The trail zigzags, gradually inclining, with a number of steep shortcuts along this section. I usually take the shortcut trails.

At approx. 1.2km the narrow forest trail comes up onto a fire road. The trail turns right.

Note: There is a narrow trail up to the left here. This is not a shortcut. It goes to Feenlea Mt. so make sure to keep following the red and yellow markers. From here the trail is an open fire road (wide forest road).

At approx. 2.5km you come to a Y junction; head left following the yellow markers (you have now stopped following the red markers).

Continue on this wide forest road as it winds gradually upwards. At approx. 3.2km you come to an opening, with a trail off to the left (do not take this); continue on the forest road.

At approx. 3.5km you'll see a narrow trail to your right, with a sign for Moylussa: take this trail.

From here the trail is considerably rockier and very steep.

The trail starts as a steep direct trail then it begins to zigzag. At approx. 4.5km you'll come to steps which lead onto a boardwalk; the boardwalk is a series of steps and level sections with great views.

At approx. 4.8km the boardwalk will end and you'll arrive at a large rock and the Moylussa plaque.

This is an out-and-back trail, so return the way you came.

Kilkee Cliff Walk and Loop Head

Ir. Ceann Léime, 'headland of the leap'

The region to the south of Kilkee is the Loop Head Peninsula, perhaps the most dramatic headland on the Wild Atlantic Way. Loop Head gets its name from the Norse word, *hlaup*, meaning 'run' or 'leap'. According to an ancient legend, the warrior hero Cú Chulainn, being chased by the Hag, Mal, performed an awe-inspiring feat, leaping from the headland to *Oileán na Léime* (the Island of the Leap). A key landmark of Loop Head is its lighthouse. The Loop Head Lighthouse has guarded the entrance to the River Shannon since 1670. Also of interest are the Bridges of Ross. These Bridges take their name from Ross Bay, and are a wonderful natural

What You Need to Know

Loop Head
OSI: 63
Distance: 1.8km
Approx. time: 30 minutes
Difficulty: easy
Route type: looped
Starting point: Loop Head Lighthouse Kilbaha South
Elevation: 60m
Parking: yes, approx. 35 spaces
Fee: yes
Dog friendly: yes, on a leash

Kilkee Cliff Walk
OSI: 63
Distance: 3.6km
Approx. time: 1 hour
Difficulty: easy
Route type: out-and-back
Starting point: Diamond Rocks Café car park
Elevation: 120m
Parking: yes, 50-70 spaces, height restriction
Fee: no
Dog friendly: yes, on a leash

PIT STOPS

Swim
- Pollock Holes

Visit
- Loop Head Lighthouse
- Bridges of Ross

Eat
- Diamond Rocks Café
- Holly's Café
- La Casa
- Naughton's Yard
- Beag Food
- Oileán Restaurant, Kilrush
- Keating's of Kilbaha

limestone sea arch formed on the headland. On this trail you will see a huge sea stack, known as Diarmuid and Gráinne's Rock (or Lover's Leap). It is said that the mythical lovers Diarmuid and Gráinne rested here, while they were being chased across Ireland by the warrior Fionn mac Cumhaill, as documented in the epic tale, *The Pursuit of Diarmuid and Gráinne*.

I have given the details for both cliff walks, as I couldn't choose between

Other Hikes in the Area
Moylussa (p.205)

INCLUDED IN *THE HIKE LIFE* **(BOOK ONE)**
Cliffs of Moher Coastal Trail (p.175)

them, but as they are short, they are very achievable and worth doing on the same day. I would also suggest adding in the Bridges of Ross, which is very close by. The Hike Life version of a three-in-one!

While both trails are dog friendly, with your dog on a leash, I would stress these cliffs are exposed with lots of bird species along the edge, so please take care of yourself, your dog and the wildlife.

THE TRAIL: LOOP HEAD

> **Note:** The cliffs are exposed: there is no fencing or barrier. Keep a safe distance from the cliff edge and be aware of eroding rocks. Be smart and be safe.

From the car park, looking at Loop Head Lighthouse, the trail heads right towards the cliffs, then runs adjacent to the cliffs on a grassy track. The cliffs are to your right-hand side.

At about 500m there are great views over to Diarmuid and Gráinne's Rock to your right and the EIRE 45 sign to your left.

At about 600m the trail begins to veer left, looping back along the other side of Loop Head

At approx. 1.3km the route turns left back to the car park. Throughout the trail is a grassy track which runs along the cliff line.

THE TRAIL: KILKEE CLIFF WALK

> **Note:** The Kilkee Cliff Walk has many different options. You can do a short out-and-back, a loop, a long out-and-back or an A-to-B. From the car park, pass the Diamond Rock Café along the tarmac coastal path.

The trail from here is a mix of hard-surfaced tarmac and gravel terrain which runs adjacent to the cliffs following their line.

At approx. 1.8km the trail comes onto the road.

> **Note:** An option from here would be return the way you came (approx. 3.6km) or turn left to make a loop returning to Kilkee via a country road (approx. 4km).

To keep following the Kilkee Cliff Route continue to the right, along the road, walking on the grass between the road and the cliffs. From here the rest of the trail is roadside.

The Cliff Walk route goes the entire way to the Wild Atlantic Way discovery point at Kilkee Cliffs and the John Holmes Memorial at Dunlicky Point, passing Foohagh Point, St Kee's Well and the Candlestick (approx. 12.7km out-and-back).

If you do a shorter out-and-back, you can always drive this coastal road and stop off at the Candlestick and Dunlicky Point, where there is a large car park.

Abbey Hill

Ir. Cnoc na Mainistreach, 'hill of the abbey'

I love the Burren! I am in awe of the rock formations, and we are so lucky to have this incredible place in Ireland. Abbey Hill is a local favourite in North Clare and South Galway. It is a relatively quick and dog-friendly trail, with rewarding views of Galway Bay, Turlough Hill, back towards Doughbranneen at Black Sheep Head, and out to the Atlantic. It is also a great option for a sunrise or sunset hike.

The Burren itself is a unique landscape in Ireland, comprising of limestone pavement, formed over 330 million years ago. This exceptional place is home to flora from the Arctic, Alps and Mediterranean, all growing side by side in rock crevasses. It is said that the landscape of the Burren was the inspiration for the land of Middle Earth in the Lord of the Rings trilogy. The author J.R.R. Tolkien spent a lot of time in the Burren and was said to be mesmerised by its beauty.

Abbey Hill takes its name from Corcomroe Abbey, which is on the south side of the hill, near Bell Harbour.

What You Need to Know

OSI: 51
Height: 240m
Distance: 3.7km
Approx. time: 1 hour
Difficulty: easy-moderate (moderate due to some steep sections)
Route type: out-and-back
Starting point: 4XQC+5HF, Toorard, County Clare
Elevation: 150m
Parking: yes, layby area for 4-5 cars
Fee: no
Dog friendly: yes, on a leash

Other Hikes in the Area

INCLUDED IN *THE HIKE LIFE* **(BOOK ONE)**
Mullaghmore Loop, the Burren (p.171)
Cliffs of Moher Coastal Trail (p.175)

PIT STOPS

Swim
- Fanore Beach

Visit
- Burren Nature Sanctuary (I recommend the pig walk)
- Dunguaire Castle
- Aillwee Burren Experience
- Poulnabrone Dolmen
- Corkscrew Hill
- Corcomroe Abbey

Eat
- Siar Kinvara
- Wild Beans, Kinvara
- Connolly's Bar and Restaurant
- Hazel Mountain Chocolate, Oughtmama
- Linnane's Lobster Bar, New Quay
- Gregans Castle Hotel, Ballyvaughan

THE TRAIL

Note: The trail is not marked, and the terrain makes it tricky to navigate. You will have to stop every now and again to find the trail. Some concentration is needed on this hike. I recommend downloading an online tracking map before you head off.

Corcomroe Abbey was founded in 1194 and is known for its stone carvings, especially the effigy on the tomb of Conor O'Brien, killed in battle in 1267 and the grandson of the founder of the abbey, Dónal Mór O'Brien.

This is the perfect hike to pick for a day trip out west, paired with my pit stops shown here.

From the layby area follow the brown walking arrow up the stony road.

At approx. 360m you will pass a trail heading to your left; this is a trail to Abbey Hill. However, further on, there is a more direct but steeper route which is slightly easier to follow.

If you would prefer a more gradual ascent, and descent, you can take the trail here.

Otherwise, keep going along the stony road. Then, at approx. 900m turn left, where you will step over the stone wall. From here follow the narrow trail as it climbs steeply and quickly.

The trail turns from rocky to grassy as it winds up towards the summit.

At approx. 1.6km you will get a view of Abbey Hill summit. Cross over the large Burren stones being careful of the crevasses between the rocks. From here head towards the Burren stone wall, where there is a narrow rocky trail running up to the summit.

At approx. 1.8km you will reach the summit, where there is a large stone cairn.

Return the way you came.

Ulster

Urris Lakes Loop • Knockalla Ridge
Horn Head • An Port to Glenlough Bay • Fair Head
Ben Crom • Tollymore Forest • Hen Mountain
Slieve Martin and Kodak Corner • Slieve Gullion

Urris Lakes Loop

Ir. Iorras is an obsolete Irish word for 'peninsula'

What You Need to Know

OSI: 2/3
Distance: 6.5km
Approx. time: 2.5–3 hours
Difficulty: moderate–hard
Route type: looped
Starting point: Urris Lakes Loop, Lenan, Lenankeel, Co. Donegal
Elevation: 380m
Parking: yes, at the Leenakeel Bay Beach, there is a layby for parking, about 10-12 spaces
Fee: no
Dog friendly: no

Recommended mountain leader:
Iain Miller; uniqueascent.ie

If you were to ask for my top three hikes from this book, Urris Lakes Loop would be one of them. The Urris Loop Trail is located in the Urris valley on the Inishowen Peninsula, the largest of Donegal's peninsulas. At its highest point is Malin Head, Ireland's most northerly place, visible on a clear day from the trail. Although not an island, the name *Inishowen* translates as 'Eoghan's island', referring to the fact that most communication and trade with the peninsula used to be by water, across Lough Foyle or Lough Swilly, as opposed to over the rugged Urris Hills. In my opinion, the Inishowen Peninsula doesn't get enough praise for just how spectacular it is. There is so much to do in this part of Ireland; and so, I have given a pit stop list that covers the whole of Inishowen.

The isolated geography of the Urris valley no doubt played a role in it becoming a thriving centre for illegal Poitín distillation in the 1800s, known as the 'Poitin Republic of Urris'. This trail offers wonderful views of Lough Swilly, and it was here in November 1798 that Theobald Wolfe Tone, the leader of the 1798 Rebellion, was captured by the Royal Navy.

For a remote hike, the trail is very well-marked, and offers lots of different vistas, from mountainous lake views to coastal cliffs, bays and out to sea. It has it all in terms of scenery!

The parking for this hike is at the nearby beach, so it is best to do this hike at off-peak times when the beach is not busy. Remember to never block local access or gates.

PIT STOPS

Visit
- Wild Ireland, wildlife park
- Wild Alpaca Way
- Oceanwaves Sauna, Culdaff Beach
- The Sea View Sauna, Shrove Beach
- Malin Head and Pracha Viewpoint
- Irish Adventures at Fort Dunree (for kayaking)
- Five Finger Strand Lookout
- Grianán of Aileach
- Doagh Famine Village
- Farren's Bar, Malin Head (Ireland's most northerly pub)

Swim
- Leenakeel Bay Beach
- Culdaff Beach
- Big White Bay, Shrove
- Dunree Bay

Eat
- Cúl a' Tí, Culdaff
- Tank and Skinny's Seaside, Buncrana
- Ubiquitous
- Corner Deli
- Nancy's Barn, Ballyliffin
- Market House Café, Clonmany

THE TRAIL

> **Note:** The trail is very well-marked by purple arrows and 'Urris Lakes Loop' signs. There are two sections where the markers are far apart, as referenced below. I would recommend using another form of navigation as well as the markers.

From the beachside parking, it's a short 200m walk to the trailhead.

Pass through the metal farm gate onto the trail, then follow this stony roadway as it quickly rises up; you'll notice it's a good pull right from the get-go.

Almost immediately, after 80m, you will come to a junction, from there follow the purple arrows up to the left.

Continue to follow the stony roadway. At approx. 640m, the trail turns right; now follow the purple arrows passing by another metal farm gate.

From here the trail meanders, descending a little.

At approx. 980m keep left, following the purple arrows to pass over a bridge and then immediately turn left, following the purple arrows up a stony roadway.

> **Note:** While this section is all marked, pay attention at the junctions.

From here the trail ascends. As it gradually rises, the stony terrain turns rockier, with sections of grass the higher up you hike.

At approx. 2km, the purple arrow leads you left onto a very narrow and boggy trail; there are some planks and steps cut into the mountainside along this section. The trail here is very distinct and clearly marked.

At approx. 2.3km, the trail turns grassy and boggy. Along this section it is important to look out for the markers, as the trail becomes less distinct.

At approx. 2.5km, you will reach the first lake, Crunlough; it will be to your left-hand side.

> **Note:** There are fantastic echoes here!

> **Note:** The Urris Lakes Loop does not go around either of the lakes on this hike, as the trail name might suggest. There are lots of sheep tracks leading around the lake which might confuse you.

Continue past the first lake, which is on your left-hand side. This section of trail is boggy and runs through long grass. Keep an eye out for the marker pole ahead, as it can be tricky to see at this section.

At approx. 2.8km, you will see the second lake, Lough Fad, then just before you get to the lake, the trail turns right and becomes a narrow and rocky trail.

The trail rises up, veering left to run along the north-west side of Urris Hill; be sure to look out for the sea views on your right-hand side. This section of trail is my favourite and a great spot to take a break and admire the views.

Note: This section of trail has many steep drops so look out for these.

At approx. 3.4km, the trail veers right and begins to loop back down and runs along a lower trail on the side of the hill. This section of trail is narrow and boggy, with a few very steep sections to descend.

At approx. 4.5km, you rejoin your original trail back down, returning via the stony roadway.

At approx. 5.7km, on your return to the junction, instead of going right (the way you came), you can go left returning via the lower roadway back to the trailhead start point and passing back through the metal farm gate onto the road and back down to the beach.

Knockalla Ridge

Ir, Cnoc Colbha, 'hill of the ledge or edge'

Knockalla Mountain is the highest point of the Fanad Peninsula. The Knockalla Ridge trail is another hidden gem in Donegal, similar to the Urris Lakes Loop. The trail, known locally as the Devil's Backbone, reveals an incredible hidden lake. Well, I say lake, because it is in fact one lake, although it looks like two separate lakes. The route also offers unbelievable views of Lough Swilly and further out to sea. A central feature of the Fanad Peninsula is Fanad Head Lighthouse, which has been voted as one of the most beautiful lighthouses in the world. It has been a working lighthouse since St Patrick's Day 1817. The beginning of this trail is also a pilgrim path, which brings you to the striking 'Way of the Cross' outdoor chapel. The trail up to the chapel is marked with the stations of the cross, and the chapel itself offers three large crosses and a stone altar.

> **Note:** If downloading tracking or maps, do so beforehand in case there is no reception once you are on the hike.

What You Need to Know

OSI: 2
Height: 363m
Distance: 8.8km
Approx. time: 3 hours
Difficulty: hard
Route type: looped
Starting point: 5c84+2FG Glenvar, Co. Donegal
Elevation: 330m
Parking: yes, about 5-6 spaces
Fee: no
Dog friendly: yes, on a leash

Recommended mountain leader: Iain Miller; uniqueascent.ie

Other Hikes in the Area

Urris Lakes Loop (p.221)

Note: This is a small layby by the starting point for the 'Way of the Cross' pilgrim path. There is a gate at the entrance to this trail which you will have to open and close.

There are three options for this trail:
1. Out-and-back along Knockalla Ridge and Knockalla Summit.
2. Knockalla Ridge Loop (section on road).
3. Out-and-back to the Lake.

My favourite way to enjoy this hike is option two, the loop, as it offers the best views. I have described this below. Be aware that a section of this trail is on a narrow and winding rural road, so caution is advised. Make sure you are wearing appropriate clothing if walking during low light, and don't use headphones that could obstruct your hearing on this section of road.

THE TRAIL

Note: This trail is not marked. While there is a roadway for sections, there is a long section with no visible trail and navigation is essential.

Pass through the gate to access the layby parking area, making sure to close it after you. There is a pilgrim plaque marking this parking spot, as this is also the start to the Way of the Cross outdoor chapel, which

will be your first stop.

From here, walk up the road, then at approx. 800m you will arrive at the Way of the Cross. Stop to enjoy the views.

Return back down along the road. At approx. 1.2km (400m back down from the Way of the Crosses), at a bend in the road, follow the grass and stone path off to the left.

This is the rocky and grassy trail up towards Knockalla Ridge. Continue to follow this as it gradually ascends: it is a steady and consistent climb.

At approx. 2.5km, the trail ends and the route then turns left up along a steep slope. Note that there is no trail here aside from some sheep tracks, so navigation is necessary.

| **Note:** This section is steep and you are hiking over heather.

At approx. 2.8km, you will have ascended up onto the ridge and will see a small cairn ahead. The route heads towards the cairn.

| **Note:** This section offers marvellous

PIT STOPS

Swim
- Ballymastocker Beach

Visit
- Fanad Lighthouse
- Arryheerna Beach
- Great Pollet Sea Arch
- Ballymastocker Beach Viewpoint
- Lough Salt Parking Viewpoint

Eat
- Burger Jacks
- The Narrow Quarter Bistro & Coffeehouse
- Coffee Time, Kilmacrenan
- The Coffee Garden, Milford

views of Ballymastocker Beach down to your right.

At approx. 2.9km, at the cairn, the trail becomes distinctive again. It is a narrow and boggy trail through the heather.

The trail dips up and down, and at about 3.7km, you arrive at the view over the lake and towards Knockalla summit. This section offers the best views on the trail.

Note: There is an option to do an out-and-back from here.

Follow the trail as it undulates across the landscape, with the lake to your right. There are also amazing views along this section.

The trail terrain is grassy and boggy along here, and sometimes the trail is hard to make out.

At approx. 4.4km, from here there are a variety of options for the rest of your hike.

Knockalla summit out-and-back:
In front of you, you will also see a narrow trail which runs up towards Knockalla summit (this is a 1.4km out-and-back, with a very steep climb to a cairn marking the summit). There are amazing views from the summit, if you have the time and energy. From the summit, you return the way you came, rejoining the trail.

From the summit, you can do an out-and-back and return the way you came.

Looped trail:
With the lake to your right and Knockalla Mountain in front of you, follow the stone and grass trail to the left, which descends gradually down to a road. You will pass through a wire gateway, with a 'dogs on lead/keep gate closed' sign.

From here, continue down the road, and at the T-junction turn left. Walking along the road, you will pass by a church and an old school.

At approx. 8.4km, turn left following the signs for 'Way of the Cross' back up to the car park.

Note: This section of the route is about 3.6km on road. On a summer's day it is very picturesque, but always be mindful of vehicles.

Horn Head

Ir. Corrán Binne, 'point of the cliff'

Horn Head is a peninsula in north-west Donegal. There are several trail options to explore this breathtaking peninsula. It is hard to beat Donegal for cliffs, and Horn Head is no exception, with 180m-high cliffs crashing into the Atlantic and panoramic views of Donegal and its islands. On a clear day you can see Tory Island, the only place in Ireland to have a customary king, where the islands choose a king by consensus to represent them. The last King of Tory was Patsy Dan Rodgers, who died in 2018. You might also just make out Malin Head, the most northerly point in Ireland and Errigal, Donegal's tallest mountain.

Horn Head is a Special Area of Conservation, due to its many important habitats, including quartzite cliffs, mud flats and dunes. The cliffs, in particular, are an important breeding area for seabirds, in particular, European Shag and Razorbill. On the trail you will come across the ruins of a signal tower, a Napoleonic era lookout tower, an ÉIRE sign from the Second World War, and the old coastguard station.

What You Need to Know

OSI: 2
Distance: 3.6km
Approx. time: 1 hour
Difficulty: easy-moderate
Route type: out-and-back and looped options
Starting point: Lookout Point Horn Head, Muntermellan, Donegal
Elevation: 160m
Parking: yes, 15 spaces
Fee: no
Dog friendly: no

Other Hikes in the Area

Knockalla Ridge (p.227)

INCLUDED IN *THE HIKE LIFE* (BOOK ONE)
Muckish (p.231)
Errigal (p.227)

This is a very popular trail, as it is relatively short while offering great views of Horn Head. You can even do this as a pit stop, as even the car park offers fantastic views! This is my favourite part of Donegal, as I love to visit Dunfanaghy, Falcarragh and Downings. There is a great atmosphere here with lovely beaches, cafés and, most importantly, people.

THE TRAIL

Note: While this trail is short it runs along the cliffs, which are extremely dangerous and exposed, with mountainous terrain. Keep a safe distance from the edge at all times and be mindful of the weather conditions and other hikers.

At the end of the car park there is an information board, and to the right of the board is a tarmac path, which is where the route begins.

After 100m the hard-surfaced trail ends, and a narrow and boggy mountainous trail begins; this runs adjacent to the cliffs, not directly along them.

At approx. 1.1km, the trail passes the Horn Head Napoleonic signal tower. Looking through the windows of the ruin frames some incredible views.

The route then continues on from the tower. The terrain changes from a grassy trail to a stone trail which runs adjacent to the cliff edge (the cliff will be to your right-hand side).

At 1.8km, there is a short out-and-back section to Horn Head Point, where you can go as far as the fence.

From here you have the option to loop back up through the grassy slope of Coastguard Hill towards the car park.

I recommend returning the way you came as this section is extremely overgrown and can be boggy.

PIT STOPS

Swim
- Marble Hill Strand
- Harry's Hole (a local spot at Marble Hill which is only suitable for experienced scramblers)

Visit
- Wild Atlantic Way Discovery Point at Horn head
- Narosa Life Surf School
- Tramore Beach
- Killahoey Beach
- Glenveagh National Park
- Glenveagh Castle
- Doe Castle
- Falcarragh Beach Caves

Eat
- Emu View Brew Crew
- The Rusty Oven Pizzeria
- Second Edition Coffee
- Casa Café and Deli
- Lizzie's Diner
- Brewbox Dunfanaghy
- Cove Restaruant
- The Shack - Artisan Coffee & Ice Cream
- Batch, Donegal
- Olde Glen Bar
- The Brew Box Donegal

An Port to Glenlough Bay

What You Need to Know

OSI: 10
Distance: 5.6km
Approx. time: 2 hours
Difficulty: hard
Route type: out-and-back
Starting point: An Port, P7WX+X5, Port, Donegal
Elevation: 240m
Parking: yes, about 6 spaces
Fee: no
Dog friendly: no

Recommended mountain leader: Iain Miller; uniqueascent.ie (he also does rock climbing in this area and can bring people down onto Glenlough Bay Beach)

In *The Hike Life* (book one), I included An Port to Sturral Ridge: this is a sister hike to that one. This route also starts at An Port, but it is shorter though no less impressive. What it lacks in distance, it makes up for in the number of sea stacks. This trail is an excellent example of the epic and rugged landscape of Donegal. It is also very remote and therefore a great place to find some solace.

Glenlough Bay, despite its remoteness, is a renowned destination for rock climbing, and home to Tormore Island, Ireland's highest sea stack, at 148m tall. Close to Glenlough Bay is Prince Charlie's Cove, named for Bonnie Prince Charlie – aka Prince Charles Edward Stuart – who is said to have hidden in Glenlough in 1746, when on the run after his failed uprising aimed at recapturing the English Crown. He set sail for France from the small cove that now bears his name.

An Port is probably best known for the collection of abandoned stone cottages in the area. Some of the cottages were inhabited until the 1960s, but economic circumstances, isolation and emigration combined to impact the survival of the community who lived there.

THE TRAIL

> **Note:** Be aware that you are in an extremely remote area; there are no shops or towns for approx. 30 to 40 minutes.

There are no markings for this hike and it is an extremely dangerous route as the trail follows a rugged cliff face. This hike is only suitable for those with navigational skills, tools and experience. The below is an overview of what to expect and the terrain to prepare for.

From the parking area, looking out to sea, head up the slope to your right. Initially there is a worn trail which passes

Other Hikes in the Area

INCLUDED IN *THE HIKE LIFE* **(BOOK ONE)**
An Port to Sturrall Ridge View (p.223)
Slieve League (p.217)

by a cross and runs up along a fence; the fence will be to your right-hand side, with drops offs to your left-hand side.

Once the fence ends there is no visible trail.

From here it's an extremely steep ascent up along a grassy slope.

Note: While on this section take time to enjoy the views back towards An Port.

This section is approx. 350m long and the steepest section of the hike.

You then arrive up onto the cliffs. From here the route follows the line of the cliffs; the trail is not directly on the cliff edge, but runs adjacent to it.

Note: The views along here are amazing, looking back towards Sturral Ridge, as well as offering lots of different sea stacks and arches to marvel at.

From here, the trail is narrow and worn in sections. The terrain switches between grassy and boggy and continues to gradually ascend.

At approx. 1km, there is a fence along the cliff edge for a short section, and again at 1.5km for another short section.

At 2.8km you will arrive at the viewpoint down to Glenlough Bay.

This is an out-and-back route, so return the way you came.

PIT STOPS

Swim
- Narin/Portnoo Beach

Visit
- Assaranca Falls
- Caves of Maghera
- Glengesh Viewing Point
- Malin Beg Beach (Silver Strand)
- Kilclooney Dolmen
- Triona Donegal Tweed Visitors Centre
- Glencolmcille Folk Village
- Fintown Railway
- Portnoo Beach Viewpoint

Eat
- Mickalene's Gastro Pub
- Nancy's Bar
- The Courthouse Restaurant
- Siopa Lúghnasa, Glenties
- Highlands Hotel, Glenties
- Pirates of the Coffeebean

Note: As you may be tired on the return be cautious of the cliff edge and pay full attention to your surroundings and footing.

Fair Head

Benmore

Ir: An Bhin Mór meaning 'the Great Cliff'

What You Need to Know

OSNI: 5
Distance: 3.8km
Approx. time: 1 hour
Difficulty: easy-moderate (moderate due to the fact the trail runs along a cliff)
Route type: looped
Starting point: Fair Head car park
Elevation: 90m
Parking: yes, about 15-20 spaces
Fee: £3 in honesty box
Dog friendly: no

Recommended climbing instructor if you want to climb here:
Steve Hodge; shmountaineering.co.uk
Iain Miller; uniqueascent.ie

PIT STOPS in general area

Swim
- Whitepark Bay
- Dunseverick Rock Pools

Visit
- Giant's Causeway
- Carrick-a-Rede
- Ballintoy Harbour
- Kinbane Castle
- Dunseverick Castle

Eat
- Bothy White Park Café

PIT STOPS to The Gobbins

I've given an itinerary for the coastal road from Fair Head to The Gobbins, which offers so much to see and do! These are listed here in order of the stops:

- Ursa Minor, Ballycastle
- Cushendun Caves
- North Coffee Cart, Cushendall
- Hawthorn & Rose, Cushendall
- Red Bay Castle
- The Hidden Village of Galboly (short walk from the road)
- Cranny Falls (short walk)
- Twilight Coffee & Bunkhouse, Carnlough
- Glenarm Castle
- Gobbins Cliff Walk (this is a guided tour: book online in advance)

This Fair Head hike is a combination of Binevenagh and the North Antrim Cliffs, with stunning trails and unique cliffs.

The Rathlin Wall, which is Fair Head's distinct face hosts lots of technical climbing routes, which has made it a very popular spot for climbers to travel here.

This place is very well known for climbers, but it also hosts some amazing marked trails for those of us seeking the views without the daredevil thrills.

Along the trail you'll see Rathlin Island (Irish: Reachlainn); according to the Annals of Ulster the first Viking raid in Ireland was said to have happened on this island in 759AD.

Another point of interest along this trail when you're passing Lough Na Cranagh, you'll see a small man-made island in the centre: a crannóg created for defence purposes. The start of the trail has an information board with lots more interesting facts and stories about the area. It's well worth reading, as it really adds to your hike.

Other Hikes in the Area

INCLUDED IN *THE HIKE LIFE* **(BOOK ONE)**
Dunseverick to Giant's Causeway (p.239)
Glenariff Forest (p.245)

MORE TO EXPLORE
Gobbins Cliff Walk (book in advance)

As a huge *Game of Thrones* fan, I also have to mention that Fair Heads Cliffs are featured in many scenes.

Check out their website to get lots more information: explorefairhead.com.

There are four trail ways here:
1. Cas Na Loch Walk (2.5km)
2. Perimeter Walk (4.2km)
3. Climbers Walk
4. Gravel Road

The trails are waymarked but be aware that some signs have faded. The trail is vague in sections and additional caution is required as these are exposed cliff edges with gullies, so be mindful of the vertical drops.

> **Note:** Caution is needed. Do not undertake this hike in poor visibility or high winds.

This is a general overview of the terrain, but navigation would be very useful in areas where the trail or markers are not easy to see.

There is an information board in the car park with route and colour details to take a photo of in case you need it for reference.

THE TRAIL

Starting from the car park, walk onto the road and turn right up along the gravel road.

At approx. 280m the trail turns right over a stile. From here the trail becomes a narrow, grassy and boggy path, which is vague in sections.

At approx. 700m, the trail meets the cliff and begins to run adjacent to the cliffs which will be to your left-hand side. Here you need to be careful of gullies and concentrate, as the cliffs are exposed.

At approx. 1km the trail crosses over a wooden stile along a fence, then continues along the cliff line.

At approx. 1.3km, there is a large gully, known as the Descent Gully or Ca Na Lough.

The trail turns towards Lough Doo and dips down to pass through a gateway, now the lake will be to your right.

The trail continues adjacent to the cliff line, along a narrow vague grassy trail. At approx. 1.8km it passes over another wooden stile, continuing on a narrow grassy trail.

At approx. 2.2km the trail meets a rocky roadway and turns right.

At approx. 2.6km it comes to a T junction where the trail turns right. Along here follow the purple arrows.

Returning towards the farm, you'll pass Lough na Cranagh and you'll see some glamping pods at the other side of it (Fairhead Glamping).

At approx. 3.6km, cross over another stile beside a gate. This will lead you back by the farmer's shed and to the car park. Make sure to close any gates you pass through.

Ben Crom

Ir. Binn Chrom 'curved/stooped peak'

Ben Crom is part of the Mourne mountain range, home to some spectacular scenery and lots of great hikes. Ben Crom provides a backdrop to the Ben Crom Dam and Reservoir, constructed between 1953 and 1957 to meet the water needs of Belfast and the surrounding areas. The reservoir has a capacity of 1,700 million litres. On the trail you will also see the Slieve Binnian Tunnel, which runs under the Mournes. Completed in 1950, it brings water to the Silent Valley Reservoir, an older and larger reservoir, close to Ben Crom. Also, keep an eye out for the Mourne Wall, over 35km of drystone wall built across 15 of the Mourne's summits.

Ben Crom is situated directly overlooking Ben Crom Reservoir on one side and Silent Valley on the other. In comparison to the rest of the peaks in the Mournes it is not a towering peak, but it is positioned near Slieve Bearnagh and Slieve Doan, taking the same trail as Slieve Doan for a lot of this route.

The summit area of Ben Crom has significant sheer drops. Caution and experience are required.

What You Need to Know

OSNI: 29
Height: 526m
Distance: 10.8km
Approx. time: 3 hours
Difficulty: hard
Route type: out-and-back
Starting point: Ott car park
Elevation: 470m
Parking: yes, 10 spaces
Fee: no
Dog friendly: even though dogs are allowed I would NOT recommend bringing a dog due to the cliff-style sheer drops around the summit area.

Recommended mountain leader: Johnny; johnnyparclimbing.com

THE TRAIL

Note: Not to be undertaken in poor visibility or high winds, as this hike has a very dangerous summit area and no trail at all for a section. Below is a general terrain description; be sure you have navigation for this hike.

Starting at the car park, carefully cross the road and turn left. After a very short distance (about 30m), you will see a stile on the right. This is where the trail begins.

The trail will pass over the stile, which brings you onto a stone-covered track called the Ott track. Follow this as it runs along the side slope of Ott Mountain (on your right) and don't be tempted to move to the minor trail.

The trail then veers left for the col (the dip in the landscape between Lough Shannagh to the left and Carn Mountain North to the right).

Approx. 1.8km into the hike, the trail meets the Mourne Wall and a stile. Pass over the stile and continue on the trail straight (there is a minor trail off to the right, do not take this). The worn, rocky and boggy trail then curves around and to the left along the side of Slieve Loughshannagh (which will be up to your left).

At approx. 2.3km you'll see the trail turn right heading towards Slieve Doan. The Ben Crom trail continues straight towards Slieve Meelbeg; you'll notice that the trail is less worn here.

The trail runs along the side of Slieve

Other Hikes in the Area
Tollymore Forest (p.253)
Hen Mountain (p.259)

INCLUDED IN *THE HIKE LIFE* (BOOK ONE)
Slieve Doan (p.265)
Slieve Binnian (p.269)
Slieve Bearnagh (p.261)
Slieve Donard (p.257)

Meelbeg with a view of Slieve Bearnagh coming into sight ahead. Then, at approx. 3.3km the trail turns right.

From here navigation is needed as the trail in sections is not visible: the trail slightly dips to run alongside the stream (which will be to your right-hand side) and is vague, grassy and boggy.

The trail continues to run alongside the stream (the Ben Crom river) and some areas will require you to hop over the water, until at approx. 4.2km the trail veers left away from the stream, along areas where there is no trail up towards the summit of Ben Crom. The closer you get towards the summit the more the trail becomes very rocky and distinctive.

At approx. 5.4km, the trail meets the summit of large rocks, where there is no summit marker. This summit has extreme steep drops: just to stress again! Enjoy the views safely and return the way you came.

PIT STOPS

Swim
- Bloody Bridge
- Tollymore Forest

Visit
- Tollymore Forest
- Murlough Beach and Reserve

Eat
- Birch Newcastle
- Black Box Donuts
- Olive Bizzare
- Luna Coffee

Tollymore Forest

Tollymore Forest Park, located at the foot of the Mourne Mountains, was Northern Ireland's first state forest park. The 630-hectare park opened to the public in 1955. The park is very picturesque, with ancient forests, the Rivers Shimna and Spinkwee, and a variety of man-made structures from throughout history. There are many tree species at Tollymore, including exotic species such as monkey puzzle and eucalyptus in the Tollymore Arboretum (the oldest in Ireland, dating from the 1750s). There are also giant redwood and Monterey pines. The oak timber from the forests at Tollymore was used to create the interiors of the White Star liners, including the *Titanic*. Tollymore Forest was also used as a location for *Game of Thrones*. On the trail you will see numerous stone bridges criss-crossing the Shimna, some of which are more than 200 years old. Also of interest is the Hermitage, a mass of stones put together to build a room, which opens onto the river path. It was built by James Hamilton, second Earl of Clanbrassil, as a memorial to his friend, the Marquis of Monthermer who died in 1770. The inscription in Greek reads: 'Clanbrassil, to his very dear friend Monthermer 1770.' The room used to contain a stone seat and a bust of the

What You Need to Know

OSNI: 29
Distance: 5.6km (if you want to add Foley's Bridge and White Fort: approx. 7.5km)
Approx. time: 1.5–2 hours
Difficulty: easy
Route type: looped
Starting point: Tollymore Forest Park, Bryansford Rd., Newcastle
Elevation: 110m
Parking: yes
Fee: yes, adult £2, child £1, car £5, motorcycle £2.50
Dog friendly: yes

PIT STOPS

Swim
- Bloody Bridge
- Tollymore Forest

Visit
- Murlough Beach and Reserve

Eat
- Birch Newcastle
- Black Box Donuts
- Great Jones
- Olive Bizzare
- Luna Coffee

Marquis, but both have disappeared. The Mourne Way and the Ulster Way walking trails also traverse Tollymore Forest.

Tollymore is one of the best forest parks: it's like stepping into a fairy tale and the swim spots are incredible. It's the perfect place to explore maybe on a cloudy or rainy day in the Mournes or as a place to enjoy an easy trail and dip.

There are numerous trails in Tollymore Forest Park:
- Arboretum Path (blue, 700m)
- River Trail (red, 5.2km) – my favourite trail and the one described here
- Mountain Trail (black, 8.8km)
- Drinns Trail (black, smaller loop of the mountain trail, 4.8km)

Other Hikes in the Area

Ben Crom (p.249)
Hen Mountain (p.259)
Slieve Martin and Kodak Corner (p.265)

INCLUDED IN *THE HIKE LIFE* (BOOK ONE)

Slieve Doan (p.265)
Slieve Binnian (p.269)
Slieve Bearnagh (p.261)
Slieve Donard (p.257)

You can mix and match trails depending on what kind of time you have and your level of fitness. The park is well waymarked.

THE TRAIL

My favourite trail is the River Trail, with a short out-and-back to see Foley's Bridge added in; the trail is marked in an anti-clockwise direction. The below is a general overview of this terrain.

> **Note:** It's worth taking a photo of the trail information boards at the car park, which you can then reference throughout the trail. Keep an eye out for arrows at junctions.

From the main car park area (near the toilets), following the red arrows, the trail is a tarmac path which leads down under Horn Bridge, a great photo location. Once you pass under Horn Bridge the trail splits (the trail to the right is a gradual tarmac slope and the trail to the left includes steps); both trails rejoin after 50m.

The trail then meets a junction and crosses over onto a gravel trail which winds down through the trees. Taking a right at the bottom, you continue to follow the red arrow.

From here, the trail remains a gravel path running alongside the river (the river will be to your left-hand side). There are some exposed tree roots along the path.

At approx. 500m you'll come to the

hermitage. There are steps up to walk through the old buildings or a gradual slope to go around the hermitage.

The trail continues on a gravel path still running alongside the river. Then, at approx. 1.1km, you'll pass the stepping stones which are lots of fun and offer another great photo spot; you'll also pass numerous wooden bridges.

At approx. 2.4km, the trail crosses over the river or Parnell's stone bridge.

The trail turns into a wider gravel forest road as its gradually rises through the trees; every junction is marked along here with red arrows.

At approx. 3.1km there is an out-and-back to White Fort. This adds approx. 400m to your distance if you choose it.

At approx. 3.6km the trail turns left and becomes a narrow gravel trail and at approx. 4.3km, it turns right crossing over Altavaddy Bridge.

The trail remains a hard-surfaced gravel path. Along here there are a few junctions all marked with red arrows or an old bridge sign, but be sure to look out for them. Along this section you'll also pass the stepping stones and the hermitage from the other side.

At approx. 5.3km, the trail passes over the 'old bridge'.

From here you can turn right and do a short 1.4km out-and-back to Foley's Bridge along a gravel path (the most picturesque bridge in my opinion).

Once you return to 'old bridge' follow the red signs back up to the car park along a gravel path.

Hen Mountain

What You Need to Know

OSNI: 29
Height: 354m (South Tor)
Distance: 3km; Hen and Cock Loop (7km); Hen, Cock and Pigeon Loop (9.6km)
Approx. time: 1 hour
Difficulty: moderate
Route type: out-and-back
Starting point: Hen Mountain car park, 33 Sandbank Rd, Hilltown, Newry BT34 5XU; Sandbank Road car park and picnic area
Elevation: 220m
Parking: yes, 14 spaces
Fee: no
Dog friendly: no

Hen Mountain has a unique shape. A small but mighty peak, there are four tors along the summit with two being very prominent: almost in the shape of an 'M' from side on.

The summit of Hen Mountain offers amazing views over to Slievemoughanmore, Eagle Mountain, Shanslieve, Tievedockaragh, Altataggart Mountain, Rocky Mountain and Tornamrock.

And then of course the Cock and Pigeon Mountain.

The tors are impressive on Hen Mountain, creating stunning vistas and a nice bit of scrambling!

However, you do need to be comfortable with heights. It can be a dangerous spot if you slip, particularly around the tors.

You can continue from Hen Mountain for Hen and Cock Loop (7km) or Hen, Cock and Pigeon Loop (9.6km), which offer wonderful panoramic views from the two cairns at the summit. Cock Mountain also offers great views of Spelga Dam Reservoir. On the trail you will also meet Batt's Wall, a drystone wall, commissioned by landowner and banker, Narcissus Batt of Purdysburn, most likely as a famine relief project during the Great Irish Famine, making it considerably older than the Mourne Wall found elsewhere in the mountain range. There is a bird theme to many of the mountains in this area, as you'll notice: Hen Mountain is located close to Eagle Mountain and Cock and Pigeon Rock Mountain, adding up to four birds.

Special shout out to the Hiking Hens up in the Mournes who organise regular group hikes up this peak!

Other Hikes in the Area

Tollymore Forest (p.253)
Ben Crom (p.249)
Slieve Martin and Kodak Corner (p.265)

INCLUDED IN *THE HIKE LIFE* (BOOK ONE)
Slieve Doan (p.265)
Slieve Binnian (p.269)
Slieve Bearnagh (p.261)
Slieve Donard (p.257)

PIT STOPS

Swim
- Bloody Bridge
- Tollymore Forest

Visit
- Tollymore Forest
- Murlough Beach and Reserve

Eat
- Birch Newcastle
- Black Box Donuts
- Great Jones
- Olive Bizzare
- Luna Coffee

THE TRAIL

> **Note:** There is also a loop option for Hen Mountain.

From the car park carefully cross the road and head onto the lane directly opposite, to the left of the house.

The trail follows the lane up and at approx. 520m, the trail meets a farm gate with red signage. Pass through the small gate to the right-hand side.

Almost immediately you'll see a narrow grassy trail to your left: this path leads up towards the summit and you'll notice it's very steep and worn.

At approx. 1.2km, reaching towards the summit you pass the first tor to your right – you'll see trails leading up to it. This is not the summit.

Keep left passing the first two torrs known as the West Tors, which will be on your right-hand side.

Passing by the West Tors to arrive at a wide grassy opening, you'll see two of the large tors ahead. The third tor (known as the Summit Tor) is the best vantage point in my opinion. And the fourth tor is known as the South Tor.

For the Summit Tor, from here there are two grassy trails leading up to the rock, one veering left winding up and the other straight ahead, which hugs around and up the back. Both require a good head for heights, experience and some use of your hands (at the back).

Be aware while enjoying the tors that they do have significant drops, so remain switched on.

At approx. 1.5km you will arrive at the summit. Return the way you came.

Going up the tors may not be for you, but don't worry, there are plenty of great views from the summit plateau. In particular, there's a great photo spot between the first two tors (West Tors) known as 'the tower', which frames the valley.

Slieve Martin and Kodak Corner

What You Need to Know

OSNI: 29
Height: 485m (Slieve Martin)
Distance: 5.1km
Approx. time: 1.5 hours
Difficulty: moderate
Route type: looped
Starting point: Kilbroney Upper car park Rostrevor Newry
Elevation: 325m
Parking: yes, about 100+ spaces
Fee: no
Dog friendly: yes, on a leash

the warrior Fionn mac Cumhaill during a battle with a Scottish giant. In response, the Scottish giant threw a large handful of earth at Fionn that landed in the Irish Sea, creating the Isle of Man.

A scientific examination of the stone showed that there was indeed a Scottish connection. The type of granite in the stone is not consistent with the geology of the area and shows that it came from Scotland in an expanding ice sheet over 10,000 years ago and was left behind as the glacial ice sheets retreated.

As a private estate, Kilbroney played host to both Charles Dickens and C.S. Lewis. The land of Narnia in C.S Lewis's *The Chronicles of Narnia* was inspired by his time at Kilbroney. There is a very family-friendly Narnia Trail, celebrating this connection. Also worth seeing at Kilbroney is Old Homer a 2,000-year-old Holm oak tree, voted Northern Ireland's 2016 Tree of the Year. Old Homer is also associated with Fionn mac Cumhaill with the distinctive leaning of the tree said to be from Fionn resting against its trunk.

The trail is located in Kilbroney Park, a scenic area of forests and lakes, with a visitor centre. Kodak Corner is a viewing point on the trail, which offers incredible views of Carlingford Lough and Warrenpoint.

Another point of interest on the trail is the Cloughmore Stone, a huge granite boulder on the top of the mountain. Weighing over 30 tonnes, how it got there is a question posed by anyone who sees it. According to legend, the boulder was thrown across Carlingford Lough by

This is such a great loop with a nice mix of scenery and lots packed into a short distance. Kodak Corner is a spectacular viewpoint especially for sunset and you can get to this spot doing a short 2.2km out-and-back from the start point, if you don't have time for the entire loop.

This spot always makes me think of another hiking community up in the area. Check out Meet Me in the Mournes: a great page for hiking inspiration around here!

Other Hikes in the Area

Tollymore Forest (p.253)
Ben Crom (p.249)
Hen Mountain (p.259)

INCLUDED IN *THE HIKE LIFE* (BOOK ONE)
Slieve Doan (p.265)
Slieve Binnian (p.269)
Slieve Bearnagh (p.261)
Slieve Donard (p.257)
Slieve Foye (p.141)

MORE TO EXPLORE
Fairy Glen Trail (1.8km or 2.3km options)
Narnia Trail (1km)
Cloughmore Trail (4.2km)
Fallows Trail (16.2km)
Mourne Way (41km)

THE TRAIL

The information board in the car park is worth taking a photo of as it's fantastic. Using online maps (downloaded in advance) and having navigation skills would be essential especially if you're planning this as a sunset hike, as there are many trails and mountain biking tracks and there aren't waymarkers at every junction. This is an overview of what terrain to expect in general.

From the car park pass through the barrier. Immediately the trail turns left, going up a narrow gravel path, into the forest.

This next section is a steep zigzag forest trail. It is sheltered, narrow, stony, with some exposed tree roots.

At approx. 1.2km, the trail comes out of the forest and up to a junction.

This next section is the out-and-back part of this loop hike.

The trail turns left up to the summit of

Slieve Martin; here it is a narrow gravel path, with some stone steps along the way and some purple waymarkers.

At approx. 1.6km, the trail comes to the Slieve Martin summit marker. There are amazing views here and a memorial bench looking down onto Rostrevor, Warrenpoint, Omeath and Carlingford Lough.

On a clear day you can see the Sugarloaf Peaks in Wicklow from the summit!

Return down the path to the junction and continue straight along the gravel path ascending towards Slievemeen. The trail is gravel with some stone steps and a fence to your left-hand side.

At approx. 2.3km, the trail flattens out for a time before gradually descending and meandering down towards Carlingford Lough.

At approx. 3.3km the trail meets a junction. To the left is a photo spot, then the trail continues straight, turning into a grassy trail, and at approx. 3.5km there is a short but very steep descent with some loose rock. You may need your hands for assistance at this section.

At the bottom of this steep descent to your left there is a short out-and-back trail to Kodak Corner, which is a narrow trail along the trees.

At approx. 3.8km you will be at the Kodak Corner viewpoint.

From Kodak Corner there are two trails to return from: the one you came down from and a lower one. 'Lower' meaning it's at the same level as the viewpoint!

Returning via the lower one, the trail is a rocky and narrow forest trail. In some sections it gives great views out to the left-hand side.

At approx. 4.4km the trail veers right onto a grassy trail running up and passing by the 'big stone' (aka Cloughmore Stone), then almost immediately after the Stone there is a junction.

The middle trail, which is a gravel path, leads gradually down, crossing over a stone bridge and back up to the car park on your left-hand side.

PIT STOPS

Swim
- Bloody Bridge
- Tollymore Forest

Visit
- Tollymore Forest
- Murlough Beach and Reserve

Eat
- Birch Newcastle
- Black Box Donuts
- Great Jones
- Olive Bizzare
- Luna Coffee
- The Old School House Café
- The Rostrevor Inn
- Bric Café
- Church Lane Coffee
- Leafy Greens & Co
- The Garden Room

Slieve Gullion

Ir. Sliabh gCuillinn, 'mountain of the steep slope or mountain of the holly'

Slieve Gullion is located in the Ring of Gullion Area of Outstanding Beauty, and within the Slieve Gullion Forest Park. As the tallest peak in County Armagh, the trail offers wonderful views of the Cooley Peninsula and the Mourne Mountains.

Slieve Gullion is steeped in folklore and legend. The Bronze Age passage tomb at the summit is known as Calliagh Beara's House, named for the Calliagh, the goddess of the land and weather. The legendary warrior Fionn mac Cumhaill is said to have been enticed inside by the Calliagh, and hence lost his youth and vigour. The tomb has been a site of pilgrimage on the winter solstice for thousands of years. The small lake to the north of the summit, Asmall Lake, is also known as Calliagh Beara's Lough. Many of Ireland's mountains are linked by stories of the Calliagh.

On Slieve Gullion you will also see the remains of famine walls, built along the townland boundaries. During the famine, starting in 1845, a controversial

What You Need to Know

OSI: 36
Height: 573m
Distance 4km
Approx. time: 1-1.5 hours
Difficulty: moderate (due to steepness)
Route type: out-and-back
Starting point: Slieve Guillion viewing platform
Elevation: 260m
Parking: yes, 20 spaces
Fee: yes, at the park entry
Dog friendly: yes

Other Hikes in the Area

Slieve Martin and Kodak Corner (p.265)

INCLUDED IN *THE HIKE LIFE* (BOOK ONE)
Slieve Foye (p.141)

government scheme to pay a small wage to the starving and destitute in return for their work on public projects resulted in many of these famine walls all over Ireland.

It's an amazing place to stop if you're travelling from Belfast to Dublin or vice versa, to get out, stretch the legs, use the amenities and climb a summit in no time! The summit offers amazing views, as Slieve Gullion stands towering over the surrounding landscape. It is also a great park with playgrounds, shops, information centre, shorter trails like Fionn's Giant Adventure and more!

The bottom park has a playground and toilets. To access the top car park (the start point), you can drive up the 'forest drive'.

Note: Access to the car park operates via a one-way system.

THE TRAIL

From the car park, cross the road and walk approx. 70m.

The trail begins to your right, marked by a yellow arrow leading up to a set of stone steps.

The trail is very easy to follow, leading the entire way to the summit.

The trail is steep, the terrain is a combination of gravel and rocky trail with stone steps.

At 1.3km the trail reaches the summit marker to your right alongside the south cairn.

From here you can leave the summit and walk across the plateau, following the trail down towards Asmal Lake, Calliagh Beara's Lough and the north cairn.

At approx. 2km the trail meets the lake. Return the way you came.

PIT STOPS

Swim
- The Priests Beach
- Ladies' Beach, Blackrock

Visit
- Ballykeel Dolmen (State Care Monument)
- Ballymacdermott Court Tomb

Eat
- Strandfield
- Dr. Brew
- Nine Squared
- Gather and Brew
- Rocksalt Café, Blackrock

ACKNOWLEDGEMENTS

I would like to start by thanking everyone who got a copy of *The Hike Life* (book 1), and to all of you who have messaged me incredible reviews about the book and photos from your adventures using it. It has been the biggest encouragement and drive while I have been secretly cooking up book 2! I hope you really enjoy exploring these trails, cafés and unique spots. I can't wait to meet you out on the mountains, on a Hike Life event or at a signing soon.

To my publishers Black & White Publishing for being the ones to take a risk on a full-colour hiking book back in 2021 and believing in *The Hike Life* books. It's a small team who come together to bring this book to life; Campbell, Ali, Tonje, Thomas, Rachel, Hannah, Lizzie, my manager Nora and the team at Gill Hess.

To my sister Bec, who helped with researching some of the cool facts and stories for each hike and at times forced me to sit down and finish my edits! To the photographers involved in this book, thank you for bringing the trails to life and putting so much work and effort into every shoot we did.

To my partner Zach for being so supportive while I have been away running up and down mountains, for days and weeks on end, routing, scouting and shooting hikes. Lastly, big shout out to Wilko aka Willay and Myla, who love hiking as much as I do, the real stars of the book.

ABOUT THE AUTHOR

Rozanna Purcell is a broadcaster, content creator and author based in Ireland. Roz began her media career in modelling but soon progressed to television and radio and has written several books. Her lifelong love of the outdoors led to her starting The Hike Life community and this has been hugely successful. The community offers free, guided hikes around Ireland for people to get out, off their phones and meet like-minded people. Roz's first hiking book, released in 2023, won the Lifestyle Book of the Year at the An Post Irish Book Awards, and **remained in the bestseller list for nearly a year. This is her second hiking book.**

You can find Roz on Instagram: @rozannapurcell & @thehikelife

IMAGE CREDITS

Aidan Fitzgerald
Images on pages: 28, 144-147

Felix Sproll
Images on pages: 8, 24, 30, 36, 39, 40, 42, 45-48, 50-57, 204, 206, 211-216

Rozanna Purcell
Images on pages: 32, 35, 38, 41, 44, 49, 66-72, 79, 81, 87, 108, 122, 127, 136, 151, 162-171, 179, 190, 194, 200, 203, 207, 208, 210, 217-220, 225, 229, 235, 239, 242, 245, 258

Sarah Doherty
Image on page 72

Sean Cahill
Images on pages: iv- 4, 10-23, 58-65, 73-78, 82, 84, 88-106, 109-120, 123, 124, 129-134, 137-142, 148, 153-160, 172-176, 180-189, 192, 195-199, 202, 223, 226, 230-234, 236, 238, 241, 244, 246-256, 261-276